∽COOKBOOK∾

SANDEEPA MUKHERJEE DATTA is Bong Mom, the nom de plume behind the very popular blog Bong Mom's Cookbook (www.bongcookbook.com). She has been entertaining her readers for over six years, and is the go-to for Bengali cooking on the web. An engineer by profession, she lives with her family in New Jersey, USA. This is her first book, based on the themes of her blog.

BONG MOM'S
COOKBOOK
Sandeepa Mukherjee Datta

*Stories from a Bengali
mother's kitchen*

Collins

First published in India in 2013 by Collins
An Imprint of HarperCollins *Publishers* India

ISBN: 978-93-5029-429-1

2 4 6 8 10 9 7 5 3 1

HarperCollins Publishers
A-53, Sector 57, Noida, Uttar Pradesh 201301, India
77-85 Fulham Palace Road, London W6 8JB, United Kingdom
Hazelton Lanes, 55 Avenue Road, Suite 2900, Toronto, Ontario M5R 3L2
and 1995 Markham Road, Scarborough, Ontario M1B 5M8, Canada
25 Ryde Road, Pymble, Sydney, NSW 2073, Australia
31 View Road, Glenfield, Auckland 10, New Zealand
10 East 53rd Street, New York NY 10022, USA

Typeset in 11.5/14.5 Bembo
by Jojy Philip, New Delhi 110 015

Printed and bound at
Thomson Press (India) Ltd.

For

Sharanya, Ananya
Ma, Baba
And the H-man

Contents

Introduction

Who or what is a 'Bong'?

Bong commonly refers to the Bengali *Homo sapiens* (Latin: 'wise man' or 'knowing man'), native to the historic region of Bengal (now divided between Bangladesh and India) in south Asia.

What do Bongs eat?

Anything and everything, as long as it is followed by Gelusil, Pudin Hara, Jowaner Aarak or Nux Vom 30. To know more about a Bong's staple diet, visit a traditional Bengali home on a weekday morning between seven and nine. The Bong male gulps down rice, dal, aloo seddho (mashed potatoes), uchche bhaja (fried bittergourd), chorchori (mixed vegetables) and maachher jhol (the famous fish curry), all hot off the stove, rounded off by mishti doi (sweet yoghurt) before he leaves for *opish*. That is the Bong's staple diet and it is a sacrilege if the earning member of the house leaves home without being fortified by it. From bitter to sweet, a balance of tastes is the core of the Bengali meal.

At all other times, you can see this species grazing on phuchka, aloo kabli, egg roll and tele bhaja.

How do I know if the middle-aged Homo sapien female I met at my child's school is a Bong?

(a) On the first day of the kid's school and even later, this species was hovering around the campus all morning, waiting for school to get over, looking visibly distressed.

(b) At your slightest smile the species proceeded to inquire whether your child learns Rabindra sangeet and takes math tuition.

(c) The species then regaled you with stories about how her offspring refuses every morsel of food that is offered and how hard it is to feed her/him.

If any of the above is true, you have met the Bong Mom, the kind of mother every Bong has, the kind that makes you thump your chest and proudly declare 'Mere paas Ma hain' – only you say it in Bengali.

Food ranks high in the Bong Mom's dictionary, as do her children who, according to her, are always undernourished and stick-thin 'roga'. To feed them well, a Bengali mother will spend an inordinate amount of time in the kitchen fixing elaborate meals in the ardent hope that they will make her spawn as strong as a dal-roti eating Punjabi.

In spite of this blind reverence for food, there is little known outside thickly shuttered Bengali homes about the species' food habits. The world is, therefore, lulled into a false belief about the Bengali's fish-and-sweets-only diet.

In reality there are umpteen other dishes, from vegetarian ghonto and crispy beguni to musurir dal with fragrant paanch-phoron and slow-cooked spicy kosha mangsho. And that is what I have seen my mother, my grandmother, my aunts cook all their lives. Scalloped brass bowls, stainless steel platters and white ceramic plates filled with warm food rested on the kitchen counter every afternoon, smelling better than Dior. Dishes with distinct flavours and simple names like dalna, kaalia and ghonto were cooked each day.

Coming from such a race, it is not surprising that in spite of being globalized with artisan pizzas and greasy chicken tikka masalas, what the heart really craves is 'chorchori'. And that is what I try to cook in my humble kitchen in the suburbs of New York. I adapt, tweak and adjust to blend those dishes in my busy workday, I gather their recipes from my mother, my husband's mother, my Kolkata neighbour's mother, my cousin's mother, a friend's mother – in short, all Bong motherhood – and re-create them in my far-off kitchen, along with the stories and memories they bring with them.

Food, to me, goes beyond a means of sustenance and acid reflux (ombol, as we Bongs like to say). Rather, it is life wrapped in a soft egg roll with slices of crunchy onion and bites of feisty green chilli. It has something to tell. Always.

To be honest, though I have always loved food, my journey has been a long one, from a techie young woman who thought cooking is blah to my current self when on a good day I tell myself I find solace in cooking. Today, I find comfort in the smell of the spices sputtering in oil and my musurir dal connects me to memories of my Calcutta home. In my twenties I would have balked at this thought.

My culinary journey through Bengali cuisine is shared with my fish-hating, chorchori- and meat-loving husband, henceforth referred to as H-man and not to be confused with Superman or Batman. On this gastronomic highway I also mother two girls aged seven and three, giving them heavy doses of Sukumar Ray and forcing them to eat Bengali food in the name of 'kalchar' or culture – harbouring hope that one fine day they too will don the mantle of the 'Bong Mom'.

In between I blog, chronicling my tales and recipes on the internet. Through my years of blogging and tinkering in the kitchen, I have realized that the recipe does not make the food. The main ingredient of Indian cooking is andaaz – intuition. Though I have bound the recipes in measures of standard teaspoons and tablespoons, do not be constrained by them. Do what your senses tell you. Only do not add cream to aloo posto. Anything else you do should be fine.

As I see it, recipes are a mere framework, guidelines to help you create your own food memories; to experiment and make it your own; to find your own joy and spice box in the kitchen and to weave your own tale. That is what I want you to do with the recipes in this book. I did not write this book as a cookbook and the recipes shared here are those I cook at home according to the tastes of my family of four. When it comes to you, adjust, taste, create and, most importantly, enjoy the process, for the food is good but the story that you knit around it is better.

This is my story, but it might well be yours and maybe even yours.

Happy cooking!

Bong Mom

The Great Bong Breakfast

Bengalis don't eat breakfast; they eat a complete meal in the morning, or else they eat luchi.

It had been a few months since I started my blog. I was still tweaking HTML fonts and preening at the under-exposed, out-of-focus picture of aloo posto that I had managed to put up, when a reader left a comment asking, 'What do Bongs eat for breakfast?' Soon, a few more joined in. They all wanted to know what a Bong eats first thing in the morning.

I was stumped. I hadn't expected such serious stuff when I started my blog. The blog was poised to be about my escapades in a life studded with lust, adventure and thrills. Okay, who am I kidding? The 'About Me' section said it was going to be about a budding Bengali kitchen in suburbia – 44.5 miles from New York City, to be precise – where a mother was finding a way to share her roots with her two little daughters through a culture of food. In reality it was supposed to be about *my* food, finding *my* way through recipes I cooked at home, which worked for *me*. It was to be about my views, my kids, my dog. Okay, no dog, but still, it was supposed to be all about me, me and me. And here were perfect strangers asking me to stand up as a spokesperson of Bong United with questions about the Bong's morning food habit.

Me, I do not have a morning food habit. If you had mornings like mine, you wouldn't either.

5:30 a.m. I wake up to the sound of waves lapping against golden sand on the beaches of Hawaii. I snuggle deeper into the duvet, dreaming of an opulent Luau. In the next few seconds, the waves grow louder and crash around me. I wake up, drenched in fear, and realize it is the alarm, one of those new devices that do not believe in shrill sounds to wake you up. I slap it off and go back to sleep.

5:45 a.m. The alarm goes off again. This time it tweets like a bird, several birds. My three-year-old is not too fond of birds. She thinks they might fly into the house and poop on her head. 'Mama, I don't like birds, we can have a crocodile, a fish or a rabbit for a pet instead,' she has told me. She is very specific about her choices. I get up before the raucous birdsong wakes her up and shush the alarm. This time I don't go back to bed.

Yes, sir, the day has begun. For me.

By the time I splash water all over myself and make myself some tea, it says 6:15 on the black oven clock. The H-man, my husband of several years, is already at work, leading a fancy corporate life replete with blonde secretaries (not) and private jets (not), oblivious to the morning pandemonium that is soon to ensue. His pale green bowl of oatmeal, now empty, waits patiently in the sink, the milk crusting around the sides. I have a sneaking suspicion that he leaves at an ungodly hour so as to avoid the whole ruckus. I turn the faucet, run some warm water into the dried up bowl and firmly shove aside my yearning to steep an Earl Grey teabag in hot water for all the three minutes suggested. That has to wait until retirement; three whole minutes is not something I can spare at the moment. Instead, I take several deep breaths and brace myself for another bright day.

In one hour, the yellow school bus will pull up outside the door to pick up my older child, the one who is seven-going-on-seventeen. I panic and run about popping a toast here, warming a lunch there and screaming to wake the child. In between I holler, 'No halter-neck, no low-rise jeans,' silently cursing the no-uniform policy of the school. The seven-year-old is sensible and obedient, unlike her feisty sister, so my shouting works. As a fallout of my high-pitched voice, the little one wakes up and starts a steady wail which, if fine tuned, could be compared to a maestro's shehnai rendition. I scoop her up, making a mental note to buy noise-cancelling headphones for my next birthday. The next hour is a kaleidoscope of rushing two children through the morning routine, shoving a waffle down the older one's throat, making the bawling younger one drink her milk and pushing the older one out of the front door with an 8 oz carton of Horizon Organic Milk and a pink lunch bag at 7:25.

In the next half hour I pull a shirt over my head, shoot off some e-mails, pick a rotting black banana from the fruit bowl, blurt out instructions to the babysitter who is going to ignore them anyway, hug and kiss the little one before she throws a royal tantrum, and bid her adieu. Often, by the time I reach my car, I discover that I have mismatched sandals or that my shirt has been worn inside out.

In this scenario, where do I have the time to think about what a Bong eats for breakfast?

My mother, blissfully watching *Star Ananda* in faraway Kolkata, does not know about the above scenario. And don't tell her. She will be appalled. Ma, if you are reading this, please skip this page. My mother believes her granddaughter should have a full breakfast of toast and omelette, porota ar aloo chorchori (paratha and potatoes) or at least aloo seddho bhaat (mashed potatoes and rice) before she leaves for school. Fat chance. But I can't blame my mother. That is what she fed me for breakfast until I was left to fend for myself.

Until I was eight, my staple breakfast was mashed potatoes, boiled eggs, rice and Amul butter on all school days. And no, I wasn't a thin, sickly child lacking nutrition. My baba did not have it easy either. By eight in the morning, my mother would make sure a full spread of bhaat, dal, begun bhaja and maachher jhol was ready for him. Baba would hop through the scalding hot dal, mixing it with the steaming pile of rice, break into the fried eggplant, furiously de-bone the fish and grumble every day about the purposelessness of such a meal. My mother couldn't care less. She is one among many Bengali women who think a Bong should not leave home without a heavy dose of good Bengali food.

This, I must tell you, was the classic working-day breakfast in many Bengali homes. Now, as the times are a-changing, there are bowls of cornflakes and buttered toast on the table, but that is not what a Bengali was meant to eat for breakfast in the days of yore.

Once I became older and switched from the rice breakfast, my mother came up with elaborate sandwiches, roti with vegetables, stir-fried noodles and the works – just for breakfast. And Sunday breakfast almost always meant soft, white, puffed luchi with aloo chorchori.

Now, as I look back upon those mornings, I feel inadequate. I doubt my parenting prowess. Surely a mother who routinely offers waffles and toast for breakfast will not chalk up points for good maternal conduct. I try to compensate by making a proper breakfast, or at least brunch, on weekends. Many days I make stir-fried noodles, a dish which the kids love. On some days I make dim-pauruti, the Bengali version of the ubiquitous French toast.

But there are days when I think my daughters should remember their mother's kitchen as one where luchis puffed in steel kadhais on Sunday morning and the smell of ghee hung in the air. Then I gather all my courage and flour to make a dough. I start mixing fine maida flour with water and a spoonful of ghee. The black granite kitchen counter is dusted in snowy white as I knead and pummel the dough, roping in the husband's help. I hand out bits of dough to my daughters, like my mother did, to fashion into doughy ducks or fish. When the dough is alabaster smooth, glistening with all the kneading, it is divided into small balls.

I roll the balls into small circles with my wooden rolling pin. I dip a corner into the hot oil, to see if the temperature is right. If the oil starts to bubble, I let go of the disc, pressing it gently with a slotted spoon, coaxing it to swell up. I watch expectantly and feel relieved as the white luchi puffs up in the hot oil. After the first one, the rest is a breeze and soon I have a neat pile of airy phulko luchi on the counter.

I already have the aloo chorchori ready. The girls are excited. They poke a puffed luchi and giggle as it plops.

For a few hours, I forget the rushed weekday mornings and we sit down to a Sunday breakfast of phulko luchi and aloo chorchori.

Phulko Luchi
Deep-fried Indian bread

Luchi (*ch* pronounced as in *chair*) is a deep-fried flatbread made of bleached wheat flour or maida that is typical of

Bengali and Odia cuisine. It is almost like a puri, but while puris are usually brown, a luchi is always white.

Hot, puffed-up luchis are served with a myriad dishes depending on your taste and the time of day. Luchi with begun bhaja (fried eggplant slices), aloo bhaja (thin strips of fried potato), chholar dal, payesh and of course aloor dom are all-time favourites. Luchi with kosha mangsho is a dinner favourite on many important occasions.

If you are celebrating, a Bengali family will serve you hot luchi with mangsho or aloor dom for dinner, accompanied by several other things. They will serve you perfectly puffed-up luchis one after the other, straight from the fire, while you sit devouring them, losing track of the number. The patriarch sitting by your side will show you how to tap the luchi's belly to release its latent heat and then wrap it around a piece of mutton or potato and put it into your mouth at one go. The child on your other side might roll up his luchi with sugar, preferring it to the meat, while his mother might dip hers in some sweet brown liquid gur (jaggery). Do not get distracted and do not count your luchis; they are more than a blessing, so just enjoy them.

3 cups of all purpose flour/maida	Water for dough
A pinch of salt	¼ tsp sugar (optional)
3 tbsp oil or ghee	Vegetable oil – enough for deep frying

♪ Pour the flour into a wide bowl. Make a small well at the centre of the flour mound and add the ghee/oil. Rub the oil into the flour with your fingertips. Sprinkle a little salt, some sugar if you wish, and gradually add water to make a dough, mixing it with your hand. Be careful with the water; you don't want your dough to be soggy. Work on the dough till it no longer sticks to your fingers and comes out clean. You will get a smooth, soft round which is springy to the touch. Cover with a damp cloth and set aside for 15–20 minutes.

- ♪ Make small, round walnut-sized, balls with the dough.
- ♪ Flatten the balls between your palms and dip them in a little oil. Now roll out the balls to make flat circles 3–4 inches in diameter. If you have difficulty making perfect rounds, roll out to any shape you desire and then cut out the circular shape with a katori or any round cutter.
- ♪ Heat enough oil in a kadhai for deep-frying. Wait for the oil to be piping hot. It should not be smoking, though.
- ♪ Dip a corner of a rolled out luchi in the hot oil to see how the oil reacts. If you see it bubble you know the time is right. Release the luchi in the oil and press gently with a flat spatula. The right heat of the oil and the pressing is crucial for the luchi to puff up. As soon as the luchi puffs up, flip it on the other side. Once the luchi is puffed up and pristine white, take it out with a slotted spoon and serve hot with your chosen side.

Luchi Making Guide

Luchi should always be a joint venture. Get someone to fry while you roll or vice versa. Or else be an expert!

For 3 cups flour, 3 tbsp oil/ghee is suggested as 'mayan' or shortening. But 2 tbsp works just as well.

The luchi dough needs to be worked well; this is called 'thasha' in Bengali. You need to knead the dough for some time, until it is smooth like a baby's bottom and springy to the touch. The best time to knead the dough is when you are angry or frustrated – kneading can be extremely therapeutic. Trust me, I know.

After making the dough, cover with a lightly dampened cloth or kitchen tissue and let it sit. After half an hour or so, proceed to make the balls.

The right temperature of the oil is essential for the luchi to puff up, so check this while frying.

Don't forget to press the luchi with the back of your slotted spoon. It helps the luchi to puff up.

Eat it hot, don't ever have a cold luchi. Okay, you can, when it is part of bhog (prasad) or left over from a party. But not otherwise!

Teen Kona Porota
Triangle paratha

Making teen kona porota or Bengali triangular parathas is not that hard. It can be made without the aid of a compass and protractor. Only, I learnt this very late.

I was so afraid of going wrong in making the standard triangle porota, popular in Bengal, Bihar and some parts of north India, that it was a long time before I even attempted it. And geometry isn't even my weak point.

Honestly, I wasn't even sure why they were better than round porotas. I thought it was just a lot of hype. The H-man, however, loves them. He loves the layering, the 'khasta'-ness of it. But I am not one to wake up every morning with the resolution to make the perfect porota for my husband. That was not in my marriage vows. Then again, when you have lived a lot of your life with another person, you do tend to do things the other person likes. Sometimes.

And that is what I did. On a sunny November morning, I told a friend staying the weekend with us, 'Let's make porota.' I tried to make it sound exciting, like going to a Broadway show. Once she acquiesced, I asked her timidly if she knew how to make triangular porotas. She pooh-poohed the whole thing, saying it was no big deal, and showed me how. While she expertly made ten perfect triangles in five minutes, I struggled with two and finally managed a bell-like shape.

Thereafter I got into the groove and made them again. And again. They started to look better. And after several more attempts I can now say that triangle porotas are easy to make. I cannot tell why they are important. Or maybe I can.

1 cup all purpose flour/maida	1 cup warm water
1 cup whole-wheat flour	A plate of dry flour
1½ tbsp vegetable oil/ghee	¼ cup oil used in small
A pinch of salt	measures for frying

♪ In a wide bowl, pour in both kinds of flour, a pinch of salt and a little oil/ghee. Use your fingertips to rub the oil into the flour. Now gradually add the warm water, working the flour into a dough. If it becomes too watery, don't panic: add a smattering of flour to soak it up, but it is smart to be cautious with the water.

♪ Knead the dough until it does not stick to your fingers at all. Keep kneading till the dough becomes alabaster smooth, soft and pliable. Cover with a damp cloth or damp kitchen towel and let it rest for 15–20 minutes. Once again, pummel the dough for a few minutes and then make small ping-pong sized balls from it.

♪   Now start rolling like this:

1. Take a ball, flatten it between your palms, dust with flour.

2. Roll into a small 3 inch circle. Smear a drop of oil over it. Fold the circle in half to form a semi-circle. Smear a drop of oil again. Fold the semi-circle in half along the straight edge to form a triangular shape.

3. Gently roll the sides until you get a triangular bell shape. Roll some more, maintaining the shape. The thickness should be slightly more than that of a chapati.

♪   Heat a skillet or tawa. Place the rolled paratha on the heated tawa and cook on one side until bubbles start to appear. Flip to the other side and pour oil in drops around the edges of the paratha or spray the surface with cooking oil.

♪   After half a minute or so, flip over again and add some more oil around the edges. Repeat this, turning over every half-minute or so, until the paratha is cooked on both sides. There will be little brown spots on the surface and then you know you are done.

SADA ALOO CHORCHORI
Tossed potatoes with nigella seeds and ginger

For breakfast in many Bengali homes, the most favoured side with luchi or porota is aloo chorchori. Tempered only with kalonji and bits of ginger and spiced up solely by hot green chillies, these tossed potatoes have stolen my heart and that of many other Bengalis. Sometimes green peas are added to it, at other times a dusting of crushed pepper jazzes it up, but it is always white, without a trace of turmeric.

In addition to breakfast, this was also favourite dish for night-long train journeys. All my school years, every summer, winter and Durga Pujo vacation was spent either with my extended family or exploring touristy places all over India with my parents. Both involved long train rides. Three-stack-high, steel tiffin-carriers were an essential part of those vacations. They would be packed with sada aloo chorchori in the lowest tier, a stack of luchi in the middle, hard kara paaker sandesh in the topmost tier and latched securely, only to be opened later in the night. As the train sped through unknown lands and flickering lights whizzed past in the darkness, we got ready for dinner. Newspapers would be spread out on the rexine-covered train berths and Ma would hand out luchi wrapped around aloo chorchori. The luchi would be soft and stained our fingers with its oil. The chorchori, though cold, still tasted delicious and it was clear that the absence of turmeric made the mess minimal. Sometimes Ma would also pack hard-boiled eggs along with salt in twists of paper which she would hand out as a prelude to the luchi-torkari. In the absence of garbage bins, the shells and the twists of paper would be popped outside the grilled train windows, the cold night wind carrying the bits and pieces over paddy fields, thatched huts and ponds green with moss.

I haven't opened a steel tiffin carrier for ages, but each time I make this chorchori, my feet planted firmly on stable ground, I feel the rhythm of wheels under my feet and the cold wind on my face.

2	large potatoes	4	finely chopped green chillies
¼	tsp kalo jeere/kalonji/nigella seeds	1	tbsp vegetable oil
2	tsp minced ginger		Salt to taste

♪ Boil the potatoes till they are fork-tender. Immediately rinse in cold water to stop further cooking. Peel the skin and chop into cubes.

♪ Heat oil in a pan.

♪ Temper the oil with kalo jeere. In a minute it will start sputtering. Add the minced ginger and green chillies. Fry for a minute. The ginger should give you a nice aroma.

♪ Add the cubed potatoes. Sprinkle salt. Gently toss the potatoes. Sauté for 3–4 minutes. Cook till the potatoes are fully done but not mashed up. They will start to brown and should be nicely flecked with the kalo jeere, ginger and green chilli.

Koraishutir Kochuri
Green peas kachori

In winter when sweet green peas are in abundance, pea kochuri is a popular Bengali breakfast. The dough is similar to luchi dough and it is the sweet pea stuffing which makes it special.

How to make the green pea stuffing:

1	cup sweet green peas (shelled)	¼	tsp red chilli powder
¾	tbsp chopped ginger		Pinch of asafoetida/hing
2	green chillies		Salt to taste
¼	tsp cumin powder	2	tsp mustard oil

♪ Add the peas, ginger and green chillies to a blender and make a paste, adding very little water.

♪ Heat oil in a frying pan. Add a pinch of hing (asafoetida). I will insist on this as it lends a beautiful fragrance. Many Bengali homes will use a little whole cumin instead of hing, but I stand by hing. Add the pea paste that you just made. Sprinkle ¼ tsp cumin powder. Add salt to taste. If your peas are not sweet enough, add a little sugar. If you like your food hot, add a dash of red chilli powder. Now keep stirring till the water from the pea mix totally evaporates and the mixture becomes dry and thick and congeals. Basically it should come to a stage where you can make a small ball for the stuffing.

꒐ Make dough as you would for luchi. Roll out a small disc from the dough and heap a spoonful of the green pea stuffing in its centre. Bunch up like a purse. Now pinch the top to cover up the opening and flatten it out on the palm of your hand. Roll out like a luchi and deep fry. Makes stuffing enough for 6 kochuri.

The Other Bengali Breakfast

While I have talked about the lavish Bengali breakfast, the one that makes a complete meal, I should not miss the summer breakfasts, the ones laden with fruit, the best and choicest of the season.

Come summer, our breakfasts back home would mellow down by several notches. The hot, humid days were not suitable for frying luchi in a sweltering kitchen. The stain of purple jamun on the front porch and the dull pink lychees still hanging from their branches made us seek more colour in our breakfast bowl. Mangoes bursting at the seams with sweet juice waited in the rice sacks where they had been stored to ripen in the damp and cool. My grandmother's unkempt garden, where I spent a large part of my summer vacations, spilled over with greenery as temperatures soared and every bush, tree and plant sprouted new life. The still air in the back of the garden, where the larger trees huddled together, smelled sweet and pungent with the jackfruit tree weighed down by its pendulous fruits. My cousins and I spent a large part of those summer mornings collecting jamuns and lychees in big steel bowls until it grew too hot to step outside.

Breakfasts on such hot, muggy mornings would often be muri (puffed rice) or chire (beaten rice) served with cool homemade yoghurt and sunny slices of juice-heavy mangoes.

Every summer my Ma would do this particular pujo called 'Jai Mangalbar' each Tuesday of the month of Jaishtha. It was a fast followed by a katha (story) and pujo for the Goddess Mangalchandi who, I am sure, is one of the many embodiments of Durga. Only, it was not really a proper 'fast' – you went without breakfast in the morning, and at lunch, instead of the usual rice-dal and fish curry, you had a special spread, taking full advantage of the summer bounty, i.e., mangoes. So lunch was 'Chire Doi Aam' – beaten rice aka poha mixed with yoghurt, sweet mangoes and bananas and the whole thing sweetened with sandesh. This was also called 'Falahar' – the fruit diet – though you really ate a lot more than fruit.

This simple dish was so delicious that after having the prasad for a week or two, I decided to go the whole nine yards and jumped onto the 'Jai Mangalbar' bandwagon. I was around eight to nine years old and joining in a ritual with the elders felt like a big deal. A quick bath in the morning and a few mantras later, I would join my Ma for this special lunch, sitting on the cool mosaic floor of the pujo room. I was young and did not care much about the rituals or significance of it, all I was interested in was the food.

Of course, this concoction of chire, doi and aam could normally be had any day of the week without the 'holy' tag and was often offered to me as breakfast during the summer. But there was something special about having it on those particular summer Tuesdays, sitting on the pujo room floor with Ma and grandma, the heady smell of incense and flowers making the dish ethereal. Now I make a fancy version of this old favourite with honey and in parfait glasses. Tastes just as good.

Take a parfait glass. Drizzle some honey on the bottom and along the inner surface of the glass. Scoop out pieces of sweet mango and arrange at the bottom of the glass. Follow with scoops of thick, hung yoghurt (yoghurt strained for five minutes should be fine). Add a layer of poha/chire that has been soaked to soften. Heap more mango pieces on top. Garnish with raisins or jaggery if you wish. Mix with a spoon and enjoy.

DIM PAURUTI
Spicy French toast

As vainglorious as it might sound, I cannot make luchi and aloo chorchori every Sunday morning. I have better things to do on a Sunday. Like, say, sleep. Most Sundays, by the time I get up after the usual Saturday night Bong party involving food, chatter and running around kids, the sun is already high up, the kids are demanding food, the H-man claims he cooked breakfast on Saturday so it's his turn to sleep in and there is general chaos all around.

A shot of masala tea, Barney or some such thing on the telly and a couple of Marie biscuits later, I can think more clearly. I suggest that everyone eat cereal for breakfast. Except for the purple dinosaur cheerily singing 'I love you...', there is dead silence all around. My seven-year-old says, 'Mommy, whatever is easiest for you. It is okay, I am not even hungry. I don't need breakfast.' The almost-three-year-old doesn't really care. Food is not what she is after. The H-man says he needs to run some errands and will grab a coffee at Starbucks.

I could just leave it at that and put up my feet, but I am a sucker for punishment. Only this time I choose an easy one and say, 'I am going to make French toast.' Actually, I mean dim pauruti. I have no idea how the French make toast. *Dim pauruti* or the Bengali version of the very French 'French toast' is what I have grown up on. It was my favourite breakfast, scoring over luchi or porota, for me, anyway. With flecks of red onion, green chilli, salt and pepper, these golden rectangles of egg-dipped bread, shallow fried in oil is my idea of the perfect breakfast.

It is easy to make, needs ingredients which are permanent fixtures in your refrigerator, can be done quickly and is tasty to boot. With a dollop of Maggi Hot & Sweet on the side, it is the next-best thing that can happen on a Sunday morning. Why, this one is simple enough to rustle up even on a Monday morning.

2	slices bread	1	tsp finely chopped green onion (optional)
1	large egg	½	tsp finely chopped fresh coriander leaves (optional)
2	tbsp milk		
	Salt to taste		
¼	tsp black pepper powder	¼	tsp garam masala powder (optional)
2	tbsp finely chopped red onion	1	tbsp olive oil or vegetable oil
1	finely chopped green chill		

♪ Bring two slices of bread to room temperature. If you are a hurried woman, like me, just pop it in the toaster for couple of seconds. Cut each bread in 4 almost equal squares. Remove the crust if you are finicky about that kind of stuff. You can make bread crumbs out of them later.

♪ In a bowl, beat an egg with a fork. Beat it well. Add 2 tbsp milk. Beat again. Now add all the other ingredients and mix well.

♪ Heat oil in a frying pan. Dip each bread square in the egg mix until it is well coated with egg on all sides. Release gently into the pan. Cook each side for 60–90 seconds till golden-brown. Remove and drain excess oil on a paper napkin.

♪ Serve hot on its own or with tomato ketchup. Quadruple ingredients to serve four.

The Long Lost Lunch

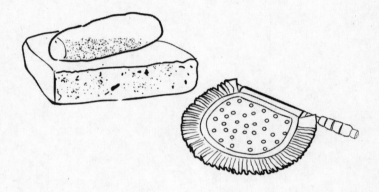

'Ask not what you can do for your country. Ask what's for lunch.'

— Orson Welles

As soon as the yellow school bus rolls out and I am on the highway clocking at 65mph, I think of lunch. A blogger friend wants me to write a piece on Bengali cuisine. Yes, bloggers have great purpose in life. I decide simply to talk about lunch.

As I change lanes and merge onto the busy highway, my hesitant middle finger raised at the black Ferrari in the left lane, I fashion the following sentence in my head:

'Here I will describe a typical, everyday Bengali lunch which you will be served if you land up in a Bengali household in a small hamlet in Bengal on a hot afternoon, the sun beating down on your back and the sleepy ghugoo birds calling from the emerald green trees. When you knock on the door, you will be welcomed with a cool tumbler of aam-pora shorbot (green mangoes roasted and made into a drink) or daaber jol (coconut water). Once you are refreshed and sit down to your lunch, there will be a six-course meal, starting with something bitter and ending with sweet, encompassing the six rasas.'

And then I start to doubt myself. Emerald green trees, eh? And when did I last have a six-course Bengali lunch?

The last time I sat down to a full Bengali meal on a weekday was so long ago that I barely remember what I ate. When was it? Ten years ago? Twenty years? Or even longer?

What has happened since? It is not that I am on an anti-lunch brigade. On the contrary, every day I spend at least an hour thinking of the next day's lunch. I look up recipes at work, make a mental note of their calorie count, and tick off ingredient lists on my Droid, all in search of three different, wholesome work-day lunches. On my worst days, I am a health-food freak and my nutrient-rich sixteen-bean soup is dreaded by many.

Soon after I get home, I zip out of my formals and into my yoga pants. They are grey, and have holes and turmeric stains. I am all set to take on the kitchen like Padma Lakshmi minus whatever wisdom and knowledge she has.

I tap my chipped-of-paint toenails, do a few stretches and wait for the *Aha* moment. I am almost waiting for a focus light on my cherry oak kitchen cabinets and an akashvani that says, 'Beti, ja, ji le teri zindagi, bana aaj paanch-mishali chorchori.' In English, that voice from heaven would say, 'Go, live your life, make a five-vegetable medley,' but then it would lose its Bollywood punch.

Silence. Nothing happens.

My oldest sits at the kitchen table finishing off her homework. The youngest is sprawled on the kitchen floor with her teapot and coloured markers, busy making what she calls 'the marker soup'.

Finally, I reach out for a blue box of Barilla whole-wheat pasta and swiftly put water to a rolling boil with the expertise of an Italian. Only, a real marinara-sauce-blooded Italian might not use Barilla, but who cares? Jade-green extra-virgin olive oil is my current mantra. While the water bubbles I chop a watermelon, toss sprouts with lime juice and cucumber and measure out Trader Joe's mixed nuts in small Rubbermaid containers; it is a darn busy evening, all in preparation of the next day's lunch.

Next day as I take a bite of my lunch, a hastily gathered salad of unknown greens, avocado and buckwheat exuding goodness like St Francis of Assisi, I continue to muse on the Bengali lunch.

I wasn't put on earth to do this, to eat salad greens like the bovine mother and develop a halo. I was born to eat rice and aloo posto with drizzles of mustard oil for lunch and take a nap afterwards. That was in my genotype. Those are the things that make my heart jiggle and spirit soar.

I know friends who still pack leftover rice, musurir dal and begun bhaja, surreptitiously heating it in the microwave at lunch time in their open plan offices on Wall Street. The effect has shaken Jewish traders in straitjackets and Wall Street has never been the same.

With the escarole greens now creating unsettling green emissions in my system, I wonder, does anyone eat a full Bengali meal at lunch anymore? In absence of a convincing answer, I just call my mother.

'What was for lunch today, Ma?' I ask, my jaws aching from chomping on the lush greens.

'Oh, I didn't really cook much today, lunch was simple,' she says and proceeds to describe a meal that starts with shukto, followed by dal and fried begun, phulkopir dalna with cauliflower and potatoes, and finally, the ubiquitous maachher jhol.

This is what my mother has been cooking all her life. This is the food I have grown up with. A healthy, wholesome Bengali lunch, much better than my greens.

When I was a child, about the same age as my oldest is now, we lived in a small mountain town in North Bengal, tucked away in the lower Himalayan range. On a clear day, if you stood on the verandah of our wooden two-storey house and looked north, you would see the Kanchenjunga swirled in cream-cheese clouds, its peak gleaming like gold in the first rays of the sun. In the west stood tall eucalyptus trees whose narrow leaves rustled like crisp paper in the wind that blew from the mountains. Behind them grew a bunch of lissome bamboo, swaying their chartreuse heads obligingly. Adorned with slim waterfalls called jhoras that cascaded down the hills, and trees festooned with ripening pears and squash, it was a charming place to spend one's childhood.

After school, my friends and I swung on the bamboo trees and picked glossy red fruit from bushes, squirting the tart juice into our mouths. Some afternoons we walked down the rambling hilly path, our coat pockets jingling with loose change, to visit the Swiss dairy which made the most decadent chocolate pops ever. From the clapboard store perched at the turn of the path, we bought salty, tangy, coarse chooran stuffed into soda straws.

By October the town got cold and if we did not shut the windows tight, the wind would enter, wrapped in a veil of gossamer-thin cloud, leaving its damp presence on the bright Jaipuri bedspread. Some time in early December, our missionary school would host an annual function and then shut down for the next three months, reopening only in late spring. Soon after this, Ma and I would board the bus with our suitcases, cross the narrow bridge over the tempestuous Tista and reach Jalpaiguri, from where we took the train to the plains, our vacation spot at my grandmother's from December to February. We would be back only in March, right in time for the new school year.

We had moved to the small hill town in lieu of my father's work. I was young and for a long time I thought the small town in the hills was a foreign country. It was in the plains where my heart belonged. The rosy-cheeked, slanted-eyed kids who were my friends and who spoke fluent English to my stuttered phrases did little to help. It was my mother's home-cooked familiar food that was the only anchor as I gradually learned to love this beautiful town and cherish my time there.

The house that we lived in had a very basic kitchen. It was the late seventies and I do not think gas stoves were popular in the hills. Every kitchen either had a chullah that was lit by wood fire or a kerosene cooking stove. Ma was comfortable with the latter and whenever she cooked, the smell of kerosene hung over the house, ricocheting off the walls. It didn't bother us, nor did it interfere with the light chicken curry that Ma cooked, or the stew she made with chunks of sweet red beets and pearl onions. There was no refrigerator; instead, we had a meatsafe, a little wood cabinet with netting all around to keep insects away. If we kept the kitchen window open at night, the milk remained icy cold. Except for Nestlé condensed milk from the office canteen at my father's work place, nothing came from cans, boxes or was frozen; my mother cooked everything from scratch.

Every day, Ma would cook and send hot lunch to school. The house help and sometimes my mother herself would walk down the steep hilly path, carrying a three-tier steel tiffin carrier that shone in the afternoon sun. Neatly tucked into the containers were steaming white rice, chhanar dalna with soft homemade paneer soaking in the mildly sweet gravy and tomato chaatni sweetened with jaggery. I looked forward to that lunch, it was my one spot of comfort in those wide halls where the matronly Mother Superior walked up and down admonishing those who spoke anything other than English. That hot lunch nurtured me through my growth from a timid kindergartner without knowledge of English to a second grader who loved school.

When I was nine, we moved again and I went to a different school. It was no longer feasible to send tiffin carriers to this school, so Ma would pack my lunch in a colourful plastic box divided into two unequal parts with a lid that snapped shut. My friends and I would sit in a circle under a shady peepul tree at mid-day, our pleated skirts hitched above the mandatory knee-length. The lunch boxes would come out – steel, plastic, thermos all piled in the middle – stir-fried noodles, plump idlis coated in ghee, paratha and achaar, egg sandwiches, buttered toast... the flavours and tastes mingled together.

Even then there would always be a full course Bengali lunch when my cousins and I got home from school.

As we showered, threw off our school shoes, changed into playclothes and narrated the day's events, Ma and Kakima hovered in the kitchen. They fried aloo bhaja, the potatoes crunchy and thin like matchsticks, warmed yellow dal with bits of green coriander and red tomato, served neem begun – tender neem leaves sautéed with baby eggplant – if it was early spring and uchche bhaja if it was summer, coaxed us to eat up the fish which we tried to ignore, and let us have as much sweet chaatni as we liked. Thamma sat at the dining table to make sure my youngest cousin did not shove the bitter fried uchche beneath her plate and to cajole us to finish our food. It did not matter that it was three in the afternoon, long past lunch time. For them a day without a complete Bengali lunch was beyond imagination; all else was jolkhabar, a mere snack.

I have never been known to serve a full-course Bengali lunch that starts with bittergourd and ends with sweet chaatni. Though I now understand the science, the balance in the circle of food served by my mother, I do not imitate it. On the day I make shukto with an essence of bitterness, I skip the dal and other vegetables. If I am making lau'er ghonto with bottlegourd and tiny fried shrimp, I ignore the bitter hors d'oeuvres that are meant to cleanse the palate. Sometimes I scour the farmers' market for little red radishes tied in a giggly bunch, sunshine slivers of pumpkin and deep green ridge gourd and I make a vegetable medley – paanchmishali – spicing it up with a dash of mustard paste and serving it with bowls of hot dal.

This is what we often eat at dinner, the one time we sit together after work and school to share a meal.

'I don't like chorchori. Can I have pasta?' my three-year-old tries to push her luck.

'Lau'er ghonto? Again?' the H-man mumbles as he checks his email on Blackberry.

'Not again. It is the same bottle gourd from yesterday, hon,' I say, leaning over to switch off his phone. Only I don't actually say 'hon', I say, 'Just eat.'

'I like chhanar dalna,' the older one says. 'But I don't like cumin in my paneer.'

'When you grow up, sweetie, you can improvise,' I advise her.

Finally, the family sits around eating chorchori, lau and chhanar dalna. We eat with our fingers, to connect to the food with all our senses. The rest of the family is not complaining any more.

It could have been worse, I tell myself. They could have been addicted to fluorescent orange paneer curries from Indian Tandoor across the street, or my neighbour's dripping-with-cheese lasagna.

And thus I try to maintain a semblance of a Bengali meal at home, but when I think of my mother, I know how badly I fail.

The classic Bengali lunch follows a certain protocol. You are expected to adhere to the order that has been laid down years earlier – starting with something bitter and ending with sweet.

An everyday Bengali lunch begins with something bitter. This is either fried uchche or neem leaves in spring. Variations of bitter gourd, boiled or fried, or tender neem leaves with eggplant are served to cleanse your system and invigorate the taste buds. Shukto is another veggie dish with an undertone of bitterness that you might be served if you are lucky.

Next comes dal, usually moong or masoor, chholar dal (chana dal) with tiny coconut pieces or kalai'er dal (split white urad dal).

Dal is usually served with a fried vegetable, what we call a bhaja. The most routine bhajas are the classic aloo bhaja, thinly-sliced fried potatoes, or begun bhaja (fried eggplant). When my mother felt particularly liberal, she would fry the bhaja like a pakora, dipping the eggplant or cauliflower floret in a batter of gram flour before frying.

Next comes a purely vegetarian dish made of any seasonal vegetable. Typically, most authentic Bengali vegetarian dishes are prepared without garlic or onion. Spices are kept to a minimum to retain the natural flavour. The dish could be a medley of random veggies, as in chorchori or labra, aloo posto or shredded cabbage cooked into a bandhakopir ghonto.

Then, of course, there is the fish without which no Bengali can survive.

The everyday fish curry was not very spicy or rich. Fresh pieces of fish were fried with salt and turmeric and then cooked with a gravy. The gravy could have infinite avatars, ranging from jhaal, a spicy gravy (often mustard based) to jhol, a light soupy gravy, often cooked with vegetables. The dishes that still arouse my tastebuds are doi-maachh (fish cooked with yoghurt), shorshe-Ilish (hilsa in mustard), chingri malaikari where the prawns are cooked in a rich coconut milk-based gravy, tangra machher jhaal (small fish in a spicy gravy) and many more. Both big as well as small fishes are enjoyed and put to good use in Bengali cuisine, the small fishes are devoured whole from head to toe while the heads of the bigger fishes are made into a delicious murir ghonto. Mutton or chicken would be a Sunday affair and fish was substituted with egg curry on some days.

To wrap it up is chaatni or a tok, something sweet and sour made with tomatoes in winter and green mangoes in summer. Of course, there are variations to this, with other fruits like pineapple, papaya and even, guess what, fish!

The meal ends with doi or sandesh, which is what Bengalis are famous for outside of Bengal. On a birthday or a special occasion paayesh is often served.

Paan, the betel leaf stuffed with zarda and spices and folded in a neat triangle, is often served to guests as an after-meal digestive.

SHUKTO
A bitter vegetable medley

Shukto is a mix of vegetables with an emphasis on subtle bitterness, a preparation where instead of hiding the bitterness, it forms the backbone of the dish. The bitter taste is said to be good for cleansing the palate and also for letting the digestive juices flow, so it is is certainly a good start to the meal that follows.

This dish is a culinary experience for one who eats it and a culinary achievement for one who cooks it. In fact, a Bengali cook is judged by his or her shukto preparation. There is even an old nursery rhyme where a young girl called Rani is rebuked for adding chillies to shukto, a clear indication of how seriously Bengalis take this dish. Frankly, I don't understand what's so difficult about cooking it, but that may be because I haven't reached the desired connoisseur level of tasting, nor has my shukto been dissected and analyzed by the shukto patrol.

Authentic Bengalis swear by radhuni, a strong spice that looks a lot like ajwain but isn't. Any shukto made without this spice is considered null and void. I don't use it for the simple reason that I do not get radhuni where I live. But do use it if you have a chance – it definitely boosts the flavour.

Before going into the recipe, I should warn you that lots of veggies are to be chopped, so be sure to get your bitter – uh-oh, I mean better – half to chop them up. And if you can find shojne danta (tender drumsticks), make sure you buy some.

1 potato

1 small white radish or a bunch of red radishes

1 ridge gourd

1 green plantain

1 slender eggplant

1 karela/bitter gourd

A bunch of long green beans or string beans

2 drumsticks

10-15 dal bori (you can find this at most supermarkets or at the Bengali store)

For the mustard paste:

1 tbsp mustard seeds

1 tsp poppy seeds

A pinch of salt

For phoron (tempering):

¼ tsp radhuni (skip when not available)

¼ tsp fenugreek seeds

2 bay leaves

A pinch of hing

1 tbsp grated ginger

½ cup whole milk

1 tbsp vegetable oil

2 tbsp ghee

Salt to taste

½ tsp sugar

꜒ Wash and chop the vegetables along their length. You should have roughly the same quantity of each vegetable except for the bitter gourd which should be less than the others. Some varieties of bitter gourd are smaller than others; buy two if yours belongs to the former category.

꜒ Soak and grind the mustard and poppy seed to a paste with a little salt and some water.

꜒ Heat oil in a kadhai/frying pan. Sauté the vegetables lightly in batches, bittergourd being the last. Remove and set aside. Fry the bori till they are brown and crispy and set aside.

꜒ Heat ghee in the kadhai. Temper with radhuni, fenugreek seeds, bay leaves and a pinch of hing. When they start sputtering and you can smell the hing, add the mustard and poppy seed paste.

꜒ Add grated ginger. Add the sautéed veggies and mix well.

𝄞 Add the milk and a cup of water. Add salt to taste. Cover and cook
   till the vegetables are cooked well. If you want a thinner gravy,
   add a little more milk and water.

𝄞 Once the vegetables are almost done, add a little sugar. Garnish
   with fried boris.

𝄞 Serve shukto with white rice as the first course at lunch.

PAANCH-MISHALI TORKARI
Five vegetable medley

Paanch-mishali torkari, or five mixed vegetables, is a very
popular Bengali dish. Didn't I say Bengali cooking is healthy
and nutritious? No wonder I never wanted to eat this dish
as a child. But right now, this is my new-found love. Quick,
easy and loaded with nutritious goodness.

To make this dish, chop five different vegetables. Not just
any vegetable, there has to be a rhyme and rhythm to them.
There must be something sweet like pumpkin, sharp like
radish, velvety like ridge gourd or eggplant (or in my case,
zucchini), crunchy like carrot, and generous like potato. You
will notice the same pattern in chorchori – again, a mixed
vegetable dish with mustard paste where the veggies are
allowed to lightly char the cooking utensil – or in labra –
another mixed vegetable dish, without mustard and with
leafy greens thrown in. Distinct dishes with unique tastes, yet
only a minute difference in ingredients and preparation.

You don't have to follow this rule strictly. I don't. I often
toss in other things. If I am extremely cranky I might add
bitter gourd and ignore the potato. But it is important that
the veggies are fresh, so that they taste the best they can –
they are the star players, after all.

This dish is my helpline on busy work days, so I make it faster and quicker by partly cooking the veggies in the microwave and thus totally deviating from tradition. You don't necessarily have to do that. Also, I have used mustard powder but you can make your own paste or better still, use bottled kasundi. That makes it absolutely divine.

(All the vegetables should be peeled and diced)

1 cup pumpkin

½ cup radish

1 cup carrot

½ cup ridge gourd (I substitute with zucchini)

1 cup peeled and cubed potato

3 slit green chillies

Spices for tempering:

1 tsp paanch-phoron

A pinch of hing

2–3 dry red chillies

½ tsp turmeric powder

2 tsp grated ginger

Mustard paste: mix 1 tsp mustard powder with 1 tbsp water or use bottled kasundi

Salt to taste

1 tbsp oil (mustard oil is the best)

Fried bori for garnish (optional)

♪ Partly cook the vegetables (except the potato) with water, green chillies and 1 tsp ginger. It is not necessary that you pre-cook the veggies, but I do it to make the process faster.

♪ Heat the oil. Temper with paanch-phoron. Add dry red chillies and a pinch of hing. Watch the spices sputter and pop.

♪ Add the potatoes. Sauté and then cover for 3 minutes. Next, add the partly cooked vegetables. Reserve the water you cooked the vegetables in. Add turmeric and sauté the vegetables for 3–4 minutes.

♪ Add little water, the vegetable stock, salt to taste, 1 tsp ginger and cover and cook. Don't add too much water. Once the veggies are done, remove the cover. Add mustard paste or 1 tsp kasundi, the spicy Bengali mustard sauce.

♪ Stir everything together. Taste and make any adjustments you may require. Cook till the water has almost dried up. Add fried bori in the end if you like. Serve as a side with dal and rice.

CHHANAR DALNA
Paneer in a light gravy

When I was young, my mother made chhanar dalna for lunch once a week without fail. For some reason, she thought my father and I needed that extra shot of protein, in spite of our largely non-vegetarian diet.

Every Thursday, my mother would put a steel dekchi of fresh milk to boil, only to curdle it with a good squeeze of lime juice. Soon the milk separated and the milk solids started clumping together like little balls of cotton afloat in the greenish whey. The whole thing looked a royal mess. Ma then poured it all out on a piece of cloth which she kept strictly for this purpose. It was actually a rectangular piece from one of Baba's old spun cotton dhotis and made for an excellent cheesecloth. After making sure all the whey had drained out, Ma would gather the corners of the cloth and twist it to make a purse-like shape. She gave a few more turns until she was satisfied that the last drop of moisture had been squeezed out. The cloth with the chhana inside was now put on a flat steel plate and weighed down with the smooth cylindrical black nora, the grinding stone. In a couple of hours, the chhana morphed into a more solid form, akin to the blocks of paneer that we see in shops. Only, my mother's chhana was softer and had a crumbly feel. Instead of cubes, she shaped the chhana in circles, deep-fried them and added them to a sweetish gravy with potatoes.

While this was the brighter outcome of the endeavour, there was a dark side to this long process. Ma would take some of the raw chhana, dust it with sugar and force me to eat it on Thursday afternoons after school. I hated the taste of raw chhana, but had no choice but to eat it. Much later, when the local sweet shop started selling paneer and Ma bought that instead of making chhana at home, I felt immense relief. My days of eating raw chhana were finally over.

Chhanar dalna is a huge favourite of my eldest daughter. 'Pan-ee-r,' she shouts, unable to contain her joy when there is chhanar dalna for dinner. I follow my mother's method exactly, but I usually buy my block of paneer. I also make slight adaptations to suit my busy workdays and my evolved taste. I add tomato, which Ma used only in winter, and I fail to recreate the taste of her fresh cumin-ginger paste, ground on the stone slab.

- 250 gm paneer cut in small rectangular cubes
- 1 large diced potato
- 1 chopped tomato
- 3 green chillies, roughly pounded
- 1 tbsp freshly grated ginger (or ginger paste)

Whole spices for tempering:
- 2 bay leaves
- 2 small green cardamoms
- 2 cloves
- ¼ tsp cumin seeds
- 2 dry red chillies

Dry masala powder:
- 2 tsp cumin powder
- ½ tsp red chilli powder
- ½ tsp turmeric powder
- Salt to taste

- 1–2 tsp sugar
- 2 tbsp vegetable oil

🔥 Heat 1 tbsp oil in a frying pan with a flat surface. Sauté the paneer pieces with a sprinkle of turmeric powder. The paneer cubes should turn slightly golden. Remove with a slotted spoon and keep aside.

🔥 Now heat the rest of the oil in a pan with a deeper bottom. Temper with the whole spices. The spices will start sizzling and the cumin seeds will sputter in about 30 seconds.

🔥 Add the diced potato and fry it with some turmeric until the potatoes take on a golden colour. Add chopped tomato, ginger and green chillies. Add a little salt and fry the tomatoes till the raw smell is gone and it has turned pulpy. If you can't figure out the change in smell, check to see if the oil is separating from the masala. This should take about 6–8 minutes at medium heat.

🔥 Now it's time for the masala. Mix the dry masala powders with 2 tsp water to make a paste. Add this masala to the frying pan.

Note: Ma uses only jeere-ada bata – cumin and ginger ground to a wet paste. You can do that too.

🔥 Sprinkle a little of the tomato juice or a little water and fry the spices for about 5 minutes. This is called 'kashano' in Bengali or 'bhuno' in Hindi and a lot depends on this step. You need to fry the masala till the oil surfaces and the masala takes on a deep red colour. Don't rush it. I have done that and there has been a difference in the taste.

🔥 Add a cup of warm water and salt to taste. Cover and cook till the potatoes are done. If you need more gravy, add a little more water and bring it to a simmer.

🔥 Add the sugar. Add the fried paneer pieces and simmer for about 2 minutes. Serve hot with rice.

Posto Faith on a Friday

Most days, my dinner is my lunch. I mean I cook for dinner what should ideally have been a Bengali lunch. When you are a mother, you make such adjustments and then declare that as the rule. It is for this purpose that I try to leave work early on Fridays. I say it is to avoid the insane traffic and nod politely when people talk about wild Friday night parties or late night binges on the streets of New York City.

'Do you have a dinner date with the hubby?' they ask me. 'Or are you having a girls' night out?' I have neither and they look at me with amazement laced with pity. Friday evenings spent without bonding with women over the cabbage soup diet and tall martinis, wearing matching skinny jeans and high boots? Dull.

Everyone, it seems, is set for a night of wild fun. And by that, I mean everyone. Even Subramanian Swamy with ash dust on his forehead is going to a lounge bar with his kohl-eyed wife after an evening archana at the local temple. I have a gut feeling that tells me they think I am a loser.

The truth is, skinny jeans are over-hyped, high boots hurt my ankles, tequila gives me a heartburn and as much as I crib about how the little one's antics drive me nuts and how the older one's repartee is greying my hair, I do not seem to enjoy my time away from them all that much. Certainly not on Fridays, when a week of outside work culminates in a point of joy and rest before the weekend takes off.

Friday night is family time for me!

It's also the night I make aloo posto, because on Fridays I become a vegetarian. This one day of the week, I give up meat and fish by choice and not because my crisper holds a bunch of rotting spinach. Ideally, I should have made posto for lunch, but for that matter I should also have soaked in a lavender-scented bubble bath and married George Clooney. Some things just don't happen.

Once I get home, I soak the tiny white poppy seeds in water and wait for them to soften, before I whir them in the mixer and think of Fridays long past.

Friday was Ma's pujo day. A day of thorough cleaning, simple vegetarian eating, smoky incense sticks and hour-long prayers.

I never liked Fridays much. When you are in your teens and friends are life, weekends away from them bring no pleasure. Also, Ma would wake me up earlier than usual on Fridays. The early morning swoosh of water across the courtyard followed by the broom acted as my morning alarm. Thwack-thwack it would go, clearing away dirt, chalk dust from the previous day's hopscotch and dry leaves from the neem tree. That was the signal for me to get out of bed and take an early bath to avoid Ma's ire.

Before the morning newspaper hit the front veranda, Ma would be in the kitchen trying to remove the turmeric stains from last night's maachher jhol. I would wince at the sound of all that scraping and scrubbing as I hurriedly dressed to catch the early bus. I wanted to be out before Ma started cleaning the rusty gas stove and soaping the red gas cylinder. My mother is a stickler for cleanliness and Fridays, under the cloak of religion, she thrust on herself unnecessary chores that visibly irked her.

When I was with my friends, I would take a bite of someone's egg roll, ignoring the rule of being vegetarian on Friday. It never occurred to me to question Ma's belief, or to defy Fridays with a stronger rebellion than this. Strangely, much later as an adult, I embraced the same rule and enforced it in my home.

Some Fridays were different. Manu'r Ma, the house help, would arrive early and amidst the clanking and scrubbing, I would hear the harsh monotonous sound of stone grating against stone. Sitting on the floor, Manu'r Ma would grind posto on the sheel, a pockmarked black slab of stone, turmeric-stained by use and age. The red and green glass bangles on her thin wrists made a sweet tinkling sound as she rolled the smooth black nora, grating the poppy seeds with the rhythmic pressure of her hands. A sliver of morning sun would fall slanted on her bangles, creating a coloured pattern on the floor beside her. The pattern danced with the tinkle as Manu'r Ma crushed the poppy seeds into a fine paste.

Those days I rushed home early. There was posto waiting at home. Earthy posto bata mixed with a liberal dose of pungent mustard oil and kancha lonka, the lightly crisped, flat exterior of the posto bora giving way to a soft core, followed by rice, dal and aloo posto. Those Fridays, I spent five whole minutes in the pujo room, muttering the only shloka I knew and promising to eat only vegetarian on every Friday thereafter.

I continue these traditions, half a world away. When evening falls, I light an incense stick in the prayer room, which is not really a room but a shrine set up in an Ikea cabinet stuffed with pictures of re-incarnations I don't know very much about. I raise my shankh and blow through it. It does not make the mellifluous sound my mother's did; it sputters and makes a shrill cacophony. In my mind, it sounds like the notes of long ago, a call to the powerful one, to thank him for my day gone past and to trust him with the days that lie ahead.

The shankh, the conch shell – which used to be a signal for us to rush home from wherever we were in the neighbourhood and start on our homework – brings my kids running to the prayer room. One of them takes up the brass bell and makes loud clanging noises, the other one starts singing the shloka her grandmother has taught her. A few Bollywood dance steps mixed with Rabindrasangeet are thrown in. Then my evening gets interesting. We take turns to thank the Almighty for what we are grateful for. The seven-year-old in her new-found maturity is thankful for her family, the world and global peace. The three-year-old does not find anything other than the raisins for prasad to be thankful for.

I mutter my own prayers and send out thank you notes for letting me make aloo posto to enjoy with my family every Friday. I am selfish that way.

Aloo Mushroom Posto
Potatoes and mushrooms in poppy seed paste

Posto was traditionally the food of the people of Rarh, the 'land of red soil', in the westernmost corner of West Bengal, particularly in the Bankura and Birbhum districts. The region has a hot, dry climate and the people believe that posto has the effect of a coolant and protects them from the heat. Or maybe they like it as much as I do and make any excuse to eat it. In the days when there was no restriction on the cultivation of the Indian poppy, farmers in this area grew poppy in abundance and posto seeds became an integral part of their diet. A mid–morning meal of posto-bhaat protected the farmers from the searing heat while they worked in the open fields.

Now these tiny white seeds are a cultural icon of Bengal and aloo posto is a global favourite. I often make other vegetables with posto, the onion posto (peyaaj posto) being the eternal favorite. Posto makes my heart do a jig and throw away my traditions. I get bold and introduce all kinds of vegetables to posto. Broccoli, beet, tindora – you name it and I have made all of them with posto. In this recipe I have added mushrooms along with the potatoes for a different texture. You can go the traditional way and skip the mushrooms and onion if you like.

3 medium potatoes	5 slit green chillies
½ cup chopped button mushrooms	1 small, finely chopped onion
4–5 heaped tbsp poppy seed paste	1 dry red chilli (optional)
To make the paste, soak 4–5 tbsp poppy seeds in 3 tbsp water and then grind to a smooth paste, or dry grind and then mix with water to make a paste. The consistency of the paste should not be too watery.	½ tsp paanch-phoron
	½ tsp turmeric powder
	Salt to taste
	A pinch of sugar
	½ tbsp mustard oil. You can use vegetable oil for cooking, but do try to get hold of some mustard oil to add that extra punch

🕉 Chop the potatoes in cubes and soak in water, else they will develop black spots.

- ♪ Heat oil in a kadhai/pan. Add the paanch-phoron and dry red chilli and wait till they sputter. Now add the chopped onion and green chillies. Fry the onion till it softens and starts browning. This should take about 3 minutes on medium heat.

- ♪ Throw in the mushrooms. Sweat the mushrooms for about 3 minutes and let all the water dry up before you go to the next step.

- ♪ Add the potato, sprinkle with turmeric. Some people make a white posto; in that case don't add turmeric. Fry for 3 more minutes till the potatoes start turning golden. Do not over-fry or deep-fry them.

- ♪ Add the poppy seed paste. Sprinkle 1 tbsp water and mix everything together. Fry for about 2 minutes on medium heat till the paste has uniformly coated the potatoes.

- ♪ Add ½–1 cup water, salt and sugar.

- ♪ Cover and cook till the potatoes are done. I make it dry so I wait for the water to dry up.

- ♪ At this point you can add 1 tsp mustard oil and stir well before you remove from heat. Take care that the potatoes don't get mashed up. Serve with steaming white rice.

POSTO'R BORA
Poppy seed fritters

Posto'r bora, flat disc–like poppy seed fritters, are another Bengali household favourite. It takes very little time to put together and I guess in the days when posto was abundant and cheap, Bengali women found this to be an easy and delicious side to accompany dal and rice. Posto'r bora and kalai'er dal and rice get along like a house on fire. A combination like this is ideal for wooing a Bengali man and is the first thing suggested by any Bong marriage counselor.

Modern food processors don't do a good job of grinding these tiny grains, especially in small quantities. I would suggest you either use a dry spice grinder to make a dry powder of the poppy seeds which you then mix with water to make a smooth, thick paste, or use one of those small wet masala grinders to make a wet paste.

½ cup poppy seeds (will make about 5 bora)	4 tbsp water
	Salt to taste
1 tbsp finely chopped onion	Mustard oil – 2 tsp for
3–4 finely chopped green chillies	frying and a few drops
1 tbsp maida flour	added to the paste

♪ Put poppy seeds in a dry spice grinder and make a fine powder, as fine as the machine can manage without burning up. Transfer to a bowl. Add 4 tbsp water to this powder gradually, stirring all the while, and make a smooth paste. Alternately, you can soak the poppy seeds and then grind with water to make your paste.

♪ Add a little flour to make the paste come together. Mix well. Throw in the onion, green chillies, salt and a few drops of mustard oil.

♪ Grease a flat non-stick pan with oil and put it on the stove to heat. Shape a spoonful of the paste into a flat fritter/tikki-like shape with your hands. It will hold its shape and does not need to be a perfect circle. If this is too hard, scoop a tablespoon of batter and gently release it in the frying pan. The mixture will flatten out and take on an irregular shape. Let it cook on medium heat. Add drops of oil around the edges. In 5 minutes, the edges will start turning crisp and brown. Try to slide a flat spatula under it to see if you can flip the fritter. Once the edges have browned, turn it over. Cook till both sides are nicely browned.

♪ You can have these on their own or with rice. It tastes awesome. Okay, you already know that.

GREEN BEANS BHORTA FROM BANGLADESH
String beans and coconut mash

As a child, I was more fond of posto and panta bhaat (rice soaked in water and eaten the next day) than lollipops. Panta bhaat was eaten very, very rarely on the hottest summer afternoons and even then, instead of giving me day-old rice, my aunt would soak fresh-cooked rice in water and she and I would have it with mustard oil, raw posto paste and green chillies. My mother abhorred such habits. My probashi Bengali family, settled outside Bengal, teased me by saying they would get me married to a Bangal for this preference. They were wrong. Posto and panta bhaat are a staple of people from Bankura–Birbhum and people from Bangladesh hardly ever cook posto. The cuisine of Bangladesh today is actually quite different from what we label 'Bangali cuisine'.

Now R Didi, my younger daughter's babysitter, being from Bangladesh, cooks some dishes typical of her home district and I can see the difference. For one, though they love their fish as much as any self-respecting Bong, they do not fry the fish before adding it to the gravy; rather, they cook their fish in the gravy along with the spices and even with bitter vegetables like uchche.

They also swear by bhorta – a dish where veggies, fish or even meat are mashed and spiced. Of all the 'bhortas' that I have had, I like the 'green bean bhorta', made with string beans and coconut, best. The recipe for this was shared by my sis-in-law, who in turn procured it from her generous Bangladeshi neighbour. It is a simple dish and will blow you away with its awesome taste. Though I have shared the vegetarian version with coconut here, if you are a shrimp lover like me, add some fried shrimp along with the beans and coconut to the blender and grind to a paste. You will not need any other dish as a side.

Wash and chop string beans into two-inch long pieces. You will need about 4 cups chopped string beans. Heat mustard oil in a kadhai and fry a small onion, thinly sliced. Follow with 5 cloves chopped garlic and 8 green chillies. When you can smell the aroma of the garlic, throw in the beans. Add salt to taste. Sauté the beans till they are soft and cooked.

Once the dish has cooled down, put the contents of the kadhai (the beans and spices) into the blender, add 1/2 cup grated coconut and make a thick paste with a splash of water.

You need to dry up this paste now. So heat a teeny bit of mustard oil and add the wet paste. Dry up the excess water. Add some finely chopped fresh coriander leaves and serve hot with white rice. To eat with your fingers, mix little dollops of paste with rice and enjoy.

For the Love of Bati Chorchori

If I talk about Bengali food I must also tell you about my grandparents. They lived in a rambling house in a north Calcutta para. The house was old, its days of glory long gone.

As appendages were added on and banyan trees took root in its crevices, the house tried desperately to hold on to its rich past.

My maternal grandparents came to live in this house after retirement. They were part of a large joint family, a term as rare these days as the old north Calcutta houses. Ma's three uncles and an aunt, along with their offspring (some married and some not), lived under one roof, their kitchens separated but their roof united. There were undercurrents among its residents for sure, but on our annual visits every winter, the whole family came together and welcomed us as one.

My mornings there would be spent in the different kitchens, sampling the lunch that each of them cooked. Clanging vessels, stinging smoke from a clay stove, raised voices... the kitchens around the central courtyard bustled with their preparation of lunch, which would be served mid-morning to my office-going uncles. Amidst the clamour, I snacked on a brass bowl full of aloo posto as I lazed about on Boro dida's ornate teak bed; I ate phulkopir dalna with jumbo shrimp at Phul dida's fancy dining table and always had the main meals in my own dida's kitchen.

Ma's aunt, Chhoto dida, lost her husband at a young age and lived in this sprawling house with her four daughters. She was a proud soul and instead of being dependent on her brothers financially, she worked as a teacher at a nursery school and lived within her meagre means to bring up her daughters impeccably.

I often sat in their small kitchen while Chhoto dida made breakfast. The squeaky-clean kitchen with a shiny brass pump stove and minimal utensils exuded a charm that no gourmet kitchen ever could. Their breakfast was simple: leftover ruti (chapati) lighty fried to wafer-like crispiness served with bati chorchori. The same bati chorchori, cooked with julienned potatoes and green chilli, would be served for lunch which they ate late in the afternoon after coming back from work. Chhoto dida had embraced vegetarianism after her husband passed away, as is the social norm for many Bengali widows, and cooked only Bengali vegetarian food in her kitchen. A bowl of fish for her daughters would be sent from my grandmother's kitchen.

'Ekta ruti kheye ja,' Chhoto dida would insist. Sitting on a colourful rug on the red oxide floor, I would readily agree. Anything to dodge the glass of Bournvita milk my mother was getting ready. While Chhoto dida fried the leftover ruti crisp on the tawa with a smatrering of oil, her daughter, Laali mashi, would be furiously peeling and chopping potatoes into finger-length and thickness on the curved iron boti. As the ruti crisped on the tawa, the potatoes were set to cook with a couple of green chillies, turmeric and mustard oil. The cold kitchen slowly warmed up with the sharp scent of mustard and the smoky, slightly burnt smell of flour.

I don't know what makes an indelible impression on a child's heart, the stinging coldness on one's bottom, the hot-off-the-tawa ruti mingled with the spicy bati chorchori or one's loved ones close by, but those mornings are etched in my memory and bati chorchori and bashi ruti bhaja (fried leftover chapati) is still a favourite on my food list.

One of my blog readers mentioned that she adds other vegetables to the delicious yet simple bati chorchori. It got me thinking, and I experimented too. So while my grandmother's bati chorchori had only potatoes, this can include carrots and any other vegetable you fancy.

BATI CHORCHORI
Finger potatoes and carrots cooked in mustard oil

Usually 'chorchori' is a dry vegetable dish, where chorchori is a noun and the particular vegetable gracing it the adjective. Thus aloor chorchori is chorchori with potatoes; begun chorchori has eggplant and kaaanta chorchori is made with fish.

However, the quintessential chorchori is the paanchmishali chorchori. Bati chorchori is unlike the other chorchoris in its cooking method. Here the veggies are not stir-fried. Instead, they are allowed to cook in water and mustard oil. In many homes, the cooking is done in a closed bowl or bati, hence the name.

2 medium potatoes cut into 2-inch-long pieces	1 tsp turmeric powder
	Salt to taste
1 cup carrots, similarly cut	4 tsp mustard oil
6 slit green chillies	2 cups water

Note: Ideally the vegetables should be cut thin, in batons, but thick is also okay. You could also add cauliflower florets and beans to this dish.

♪ In a heavy-bottomed deep pan heat 2 tsp mustard oil. When the oil is hot, add the green chilli and wait for it to sizzle and hiss.

♪ Add all the vegetables. Add turmeric powder, salt to taste and mix well. Add 1½–2 cups water and mix well. Cover and cook without stirring until the vegetables are cooked and the water has dried up. If you like, add more water for cooking.

♪ Once done, drizzle 2 tsp mustard oil on top before serving.

The Paanch-phoron Tales

Paanch-phoron, the Sorceress of Spices. Paanch-phoron, also known as panchpuran or punchpuram, is a classic Bengali spice blend typically consisting of five spices in equal measure. It is used mostly in Bengali and Odia cuisines.

The five spices that make up paanch-phoron are:

Fenugreek (methi) – the golden bitter one

Nigella seed (kalonji) – the tiny, jet-black one

Mustard seed (rai or shorshe) – the black or white one

Fennel seed (saunf or mouri) – the sweet, greenish one

Cumin seed (jeere) – the buff coloured, fragrant one

Sometimes radhuni (a strong spice that looks like celery seeds) is used in place of mustard seed. But my paanch-phoron always has mustard seeds.

The rambling house that my grandparents lived in is now in rubble. The ashwhathha tree has spread its thousand roots where my Dida's kitchen once stood. My grandmother is no more. My daughter tells me she must have become an angel. I am sure she has.

If I were to trace my love for food, it would follow a trail that goes back to my Dida and Dadu. My grandfather loved to eat and Dida, with her petite frame, silver hair parted down the middle and betel-juice-stained mouth, loved to cook.

She would spend an inordinate amount of time in the kitchen, taking breaks only to make paan, her only addiction.

Sitting on her low stool in the pantry beneath the staircase, Dida would take freshly washed, heart-shaped betel leaves and slather choon, slaked lime paste, on them. With her nutcracker she cut pale brown areca nuts into tiny pieces. Putting the areca nut and a pinch of zarda on the betel leaf, she would fold the leaf into a neat triangular packet. She would continue this process in a regular rhythmic motion with the rest of the leaves, making more paan, until her silver box, the paaner dabor, was filled with identical green triangular packets.

My job was to carry the silver box to my grandfather, who would sit in the outside living room with all the older men in the neighbourhood engaged in a loud discussion, endless cups of tea and a steady supply of paan. There was also an evening session of adda, which was more in demand because along with tea, it held the promise of kochuri or chop painstakingly made by my Dida.

In winter, when the first flush of fresh sweet green peas flooded the markets, my Dida would make koraishutir kochuri for those evenings of adda. Making them needed a little preparation. Soon after lunch Dida would climb three flights of stairs to the terrace where the winter sun cast a warm glow. My mother, a couple of aunts, cousins and I would follow. We would spread out coloured maadur and settle down, our feet stretched out on the reed rugs. Sitting there, we would shell the tender peas from their fleshy, pale green pods, biting on their sweetness every now and then. Other mashis would join us. They would passionately discuss Uttam Kumar's new movie, discuss the third aunt's daughter-in-law and complain about the peas this year not being as sweet as those in their childhood. I would wander off to perch myself on a stack of loose red bricks and peer over the high railing to watch the busy road below where men on bicycles carried heavenly liquid notun gur in earthen pots and sweet balls of rice crispies, their seller shouting 'Joynagar er Moa chai… M-o-a' in a raspy voice. When the cold winds from the north rustled through the glossy leaves of the jackfruit tree in the garden and the shadows from the railing stretched long enough to reach the jar of pickles kept out for sunning, we knew it was time to go down to the warm kitchen.

By then there was a huge mound of empty green pods in the basket. In contrast, the shelled peas seemed much less, a result of our snacking on them. Dida never minded. For her the journey, the joys shared in preparation and cooking, was as enjoyable as the end product.

As the years went by and I grew older, I saw my grandfather's cronies dwindle as illness or other reasons took them away. Dadu turned to religion and spent a lot of time in the nearby Ramakrishna Mission.

But Dida remained the same. She continued cooking, if not for her husband's friends then for her grandchildren and their friends. She is the one I associate with chingri'r cutlet, big tiger prawns spiced and fried in batter; or khasta kochuri, the kind she would make enough of for us to carry home at the end of our vacation; or murki, the sweet that she would make jarfuls of in anticipation of our winter visit.

She cooked with her heart, her hands and her senses, never consulting a cookbook in the process. Her nimble fingers, slightly gnarled with age, would deftly fly around her spice box, each holding a potent and powerful secret. Sitting on her raised wooden piri in front of the coal unoon, a pinch of hing held lightly between her thumb and forefinger, gently chopped pieces of ginger scooped up in her palm, my Dida would be on a roll. Sometimes we sat around her, awed by those hands that moved swift and deft, creating magic; secretly appalled by the mess of spices around her.

Her fingers were always smudged yellow with turmeric, her sari damp with the smell of woody cumin, the corner of her nails perpetually stained to a fragrant brown. Now that I think of her, that is the image that comes to mind – slightly damp, musky, a dull saffron yellow like the robes of an austere monk, my reed-thin Dida pottering around in the kitchen.

Dida never taught me how to cook. My mother didn't either. Cooking was not thought of as glamorous in our family. It wasn't taught, it was a necessity of adult life. Instead they all told me to study and 'become something'. What that something was remained vague, yet I knew it was something that could only be achieved by years of academic study.

So beyond shelling peas or rolling narkel naru, I was rarely around Dida in the kitchen. But at night, when I slept beside her and she crafted stories for me, she also talked about food. About how her father would send her boxes of juicy lyangra mangoes every summer, how many rosogolla my grandfather ate in one go, how he brought home random strangers and asked her to fry vegetable chop for them on winter evenings. She did not share recipes and I never asked. I assumed she would always be there if I wanted to eat something.

It was only much later that I learned things don't always remain the same.

Not a Dull Day

According to Wikipedia, dal is a preparation of pulses (dried lentils, peas or beans) which have been stripped of their outer hulls and split. It also refers to the thick stew prepared from these, an important part of Indian, Nepali, Pakistani, Sri Lankan and Bangladeshi cuisine.

For me, it is a way of life.

Just like Dida, my mother, though she cooked a lot and was very good at it, didn't think of cooking as an art that had to be taught. Her generation, deprived of Food Network, believed that cooking required a natural instinct, just like 'bum washing'. Some things are just not taught.

Ma cooked like her mother did, learning through trial-and-error, using her sense of andaaz, relying solely on her fingers to decide the right amount of spice. Scoffing at teaspoons, tablespoons, cups, measuring cans and any form of metric or non-metric measuring instruments, my mother assumed I would pick it up along the way like she had from her mother. She clearly harboured great expectations. To my credit I made a decent omelette and thought that was the pinnacle of haute cuisine.

So it was no surprise that I really started appreciating the simple dal when I moved out of the comfort of my Ma's home-cooked meals to the friendly but hitherto alien neighbourhoods of Mumbai. After a day of work and office cafeteria food that ranged from the highly sought-after biryani to a watery dal, dinner was an affair my flatmate and I assembled in a tiny kitchen with a gas stove, a kadhai and the ubiquitous Hawkins pressure cooker. Most days the menu was the very simple dal and rice. This was because we did not know any better.

The pressure cooker, which we used most for cooking dal, was also the one instrument we were very afraid of. We would rinse the lentils in running water, put them in the cooker with a generous sprinkle of turmeric, put the cooker on the little stove, light it up with a click and then run for our lives. 'Jai Hanuman Gyaan Gun Sagar' we chanted, trying fervently to remember lines from *Hanuman Chalisa* while the cooker hissed and whistled and we waited with bated breath for it to burst at any time.

If you really must know, the fact that a pressure cooker might burst is an ingrained fear in the heart of many an unsuspecting Bong child, the phrase having been uttered with serious conviction by her ma, kakima, jethima, para'r kakima for ages. There is little you can do when your childhood has been fraught with such dark premonitions.

Amazingly, the pressure cooker never lived up to its reputation. It never burst. After the mandatory three harsh whistles, we would tiptoe around it and with a swift sweep of the hand, click off the stove. The cooker would then hiss mildly, slightly dejected at being obstructed on its adventurous path. Gradually it would give up hissing altogether and we would safely approach it, tugging at its handles, finally opening it to reveal a sea of yellow cooked lentils.

We would then do the tadka, the tempering, the putting of life-and-spice into the dal. If it was my non-Bengali friend's tadka day, the process would start with heating up ghee in a small kadhai, tempering the hot, liquid gold ghee with a chaunk of cumin seeds and garlic, pouring the now flavoured ghee into the dal and then mixing, urging the dal to soak up what the ghee and spices offered.

Later I have seen my friends using a small ladle with a long handle which they use to do the chaunk and have found it irresistibly cute. I have always imagined myself doing a tadka of cumin seeds and garlic in that sexy way. But I haven't. I always go back to my Ma's methods and follow the Bengali way.

On the days we followed the Bengali process, we would start off with heating mustard oil in a big kadhai. Then we would temper the hot oil, this time with the tiny black seeds of kalonji and a couple of slit, shiny green chillies. When the kalonji danced around merrily, throwing a fit like a two-year-old on caffeine, we would pour the pressure-cooked dal into it. There would be a lot of sizzling and spattering as the dal met its match in the phoron. We would then let the dal bubble merrily, adding salt and sugar as required. Most days the dal would be a musuri'r dal for me or a toor dal for her. I don't remember ever making any other kind.

The silky, smooth dal ladled over steaming white rice sent a warm bolt of sunshine through us.

As I grew older, I made friends with the yellow moong, the gray-white kalai and the sturdy chana. Winter saw me roasting moong to a nutty aroma and making a bhaja mung'er dal with peas and cauliflower. The golden yellow dal brought back the warmth of patterned quilts sunned on the terrace on winter afternoons. On the days I had guests over I made sure that a chholar dal bubbled on the stove, garnished with small coconut pieces. I made a kalai'er dal with a phoron of mouri (fennel) along with aloo posto on hot summer days. Those white lentils reminded me of cool red oxide floors with black borders. And on days when I sought nothing but comfort, I cooked a yellow musuri'r dal, my first dal love.

Bhaja Mung'er Dal
Roasted Yellow Moong with Cauliflower and Shrimp

Bhaja Mung'er Dal or a dal where the lentils are dry roasted and then cooked is a sombre dal. It demands attention and respect and likes to be served on occasions that require rustling silk and embroidered blouses. It is usually a winter dal and this is the season my Ma would make it with cauliflowers and sweet green peas. If I could trap winter fragrance in a bottle, then buried deep in the smells of naphthalene-scented Kashmiri shawls and a foggy morning would be the smell of the roasting moong dal. It is usually cooked with sweet green peas and cauliflower to mark a vegetarian beginning, but here I have added some shrimp to make it more widely appealing than it ever aspired to be.

1½ cup yellow moong dal	**Whole spices for tempering:**
10–12 small cauliflower florets	1 tsp cumin seeds
10–12 medium sized shrimp, peeled and deveined (optional)	2 small bay leaves
	1" thin cinnamon stick
¼ cup peas (if not using shrimp)	3 dry red chillies
1 heaped tsp fresh grated ginger	
	1 tsp turmeric powder
	1 tsp sugar
	Salt to taste
	1 tbsp vegetable oil
	1 tsp ghee

♪ Dry roast the yellow moong dal for 5–6 minutes at medium heat. As soon as 50 per cent of the dal has taken on a brown shade, switch off the stove. You should not burn the dal in the process. You know it is done when you get a nice, warm, roasted nutty aroma.

Note: Dry roast means that you do not use oil, but roast it dry. Rinse the roasted dal gently in cold water.

♪ You can cook the dal in two ways. If using a pressure cooker, put the roasted lentils in the cooker with double the amount of water and a ½ tsp turmeric powder. Cook for 3–4 minutes at full pressure.

♪ If you are not using the cooker, put the dal in a pot with about 4 cups of water and add a little turmeric. Let it cook. When the dal bubbles and froths, skim the froth. Add more water if necessary and cook till the lentils are soft and edible, but not mushy. This will take a good half-hour.

Now to the tempering.

♪ Clean and devein shrimp, sprinkle salt and keep aside for 5 minutes. Chop half of a cauliflower in small florets.

♪ Heat 1 tsp oil in a soup pot/kadhai. Fry the shrimp with a little turmeric. As soon as they turn a light orange, remove and keep aside. Fry the cauliflower florets with a sprinkle of turmeric powder till they get little brown spots, then remove and keep aside.

♪ Add the rest of the oil and ½ tsp ghee to the pot. Temper the oil with the whole spices.

♪ When the spices sputter, add the ginger. Sauté for half a minute and add the cooked dal. Do not add any dal water at this point. Fry the dal for about 2–3 minutes.

♪ Now add about 2 cups of water and salt to taste. Add the cauliflower and peas. Let it simmer and come to a boil. Cook till cauliflower is done. Add ½ tsp sugar and mix. Add the shrimp, mix and switch off the stove.

🌶 Stir in the rest of the ghee and let the dal sit for 10 minutes to soak in the flavours before serving.

🌶 I like a slight hint of lime in my dal and so I add a tsp lime juice. This is definitely optional but lends a nice touch. Eat this dal as a soup or with white rice.

I often take liberties and play around with my dal. Once you are comfortable with something I think you should do that too. Switch around the ingredients, add something, and substitute something else. A dal will not disappoint you.

The Other Chholar Dal

It was a Saturday that did not dawn right.

I usually like Saturdays better than Sundays.

Most Saturday mornings I am perky and relaxed and am successful at delegating breakfast chores to the H-man. That leaves me enough time to sleep in and then panic about ferrying one kid to piano and the other to her Mommy & Me class.

But this Saturday I had a premonition that things would not be the same. For one, I got up early; just like that, without little humans jumping on me or poking my eyes with sharp objects. This was a miracle in itself and warranted a whole ten dollars' worth of archana. Then I logged onto my blog to check what people had to say about the chholar dal that I had posted earlier that week and guess what? There wasn't a single nasty comment from a single nasty troll. There wasn't even a spammer asking me to visit Niagara or buy Viagra.

This was unusual. In the recipe that I had posted on my blog, I had replaced coconut pieces with almonds because my pantry lacked the former. I had expected some serious comments admonishing my frivolity. Bongs take their chholar dal pretty seriously and it is not every day that they see someone messing up the traditional ingredients. Since I thrive on the comments on my blog, making up imaginary dialogues with the virtual commentators, I was fully geared to take on anyone who dared snub my chholar dal. 'Dude, my dal, my way', was the sharp retort I had in mind. I had even mumbled it a couple of times in a low voice with the right pause at the commas. But all I could do was write 'Thank You ☺ Hugs' to the thirty people who said 'Awesome, nice dal'.

This 'goodness of the human heart' left me very crabby and I was mulling over whether anyone really reads what I write when my musings were interrupted by my friend N's call.

Her flashing number reminded me that I had totally forgotten about the chholar dal I had promised to take for dinner at her place that evening. It is not in my nature to go around offering such things and I do not know under what circumstances I had made such a lofty promise. So it was no surprise that I had forgotten all about it.

Even as I picked up the phone, I frantically rummaged around in the over-loaded pantry, searching for the elusive packet of dried coconut pieces. I did not want to face a Bong mashima with my almond-loaded dal after all.

N did not go the coconut route though. She asked me if I had a recipe for chholar dal with garlic and onion. I was shocked. Yes, not 'mildly surprised' – shocked. There was only one kind of chholar dal I knew, a shuddha niramish one, which I cooked maybe twice a year and I could swear that it had nary a whiff of garlic or onion. Heck, I thought chholar dal had to be totally niramish, no onion, no garlic.

'But your mom makes it,' my friend said. 'She made it for your daughter's fifth birthday and it tasted like the chholar dal served at weddings. She said she had added a little garlic and onion.'

It had been two years since the birthday, more than ten since I had attended any Bengali wedding and I did not remember anything close to what she was describing.

'Ask her, get the recipe and bring that one today,' the friend said, a subtle threat in her voice. That was what made me call my mom four seconds later.

Before I go into what happened next, I should explain the synergy between my mom and dal.

My mom makes one hundred and fifty different kinds of dals. Actually that is an understatement. Frankly, I do not know how many different kinds she makes.

Every time she cooks a dal, she uses a different phoron, adds an onion here, removes a garlic there and thus creates a new end product. A product that might look familiar, but when you take a spoonful, voila! A whole different taste assaults your senses.

Take the case of musuri'r dal. We always use either paanch-phoron or kalonji as phoron for a masoor dal. Sometimes an onion is added, sometimes not. This is the limit of my innovation. But my mom goes ahead and uses a phoron of methi seeds and hing, throwing totally foreign flavours in the same dal. It is like Nirupa Roy in jeans or at least a halter neck blouse.

Sometimes you accept the new taste and move on, sometimes you fall irrevocably in love with the new avatar, and sometimes all you want is comfort and you say, 'Mujhe meri dal waapas do.'

Since she makes so many different kinds, all I do when she is here is eat and never ask a question other than 'Ki phoron dile?' (What tempering did you give?). I only ask this out of natural human curiosity. Most of the time I do not retain the information she gives in response.

Later in the day, I hollered over the phone, 'Ma, what is that chholar dal you make with onion and garlic which N loved? Give me the recipe.'

My mom said, 'Garlic... garlic? I added onion, but did I add garlic?'

How was I supposed to know? Here was someone who had eaten the dal two years ago and said that it had garlic. Here was my mom, who in the two years since had probably made multiple variations of the same dal and was now tripping over the garlic part of the recipe.

So she gave me a recipe with onion et al but no garlic.

Ten minutes later she called to suggest that I put in a tiny clove of finely minced garlic.

Now if you are not a Bengali you might get confused about all this discussion over a bit of garlic. For you, it probably has no significance in the greater scheme of things. But for us, putting garlic in chholar dal is a big deal. You need a certain braveness of heart to do it, to step over all those niramish dals cooked in the Bong kitchen for centuries and then go and put something like Allium sativum (aka garlic) and mess up the balance of the universe.

But I did just that. I used a tiny clove, the smallest in the huge bulbs I get here. It didn't make a whole lot of difference. The chholar dal tasted beautiful, better than the usual one I make, but I could barely smell the garlic in it. Really, you need to increase the dosage a bit if you want a spicier version. This worked best for us and I will probably be making this more often than the standard one.

N said it wasn't exactly like my mom's, it fell about two notches below the standard she had set. But isn't that how it always is?

Onyo Chholar Dal
Chholar dal with garlic

1 cup chana dal/chholar dal	1 tbsp ginger, minced
	1 small tomato, pureed
Spices for tempering:	¼ tsp hing/asafoetida
1 small bay leaf	½ tsp turmeric powder
3 green cardamom	¼ tsp red chilli powder
3 clove	Salt to taste
1 cinnamon stick	½ tsp sugar
2 whole dried red chillies	1 tbsp vegetable oil
⅓ cup onion, finely chopped	1 tsp ghee
1 clove garlic, minced	

- ♪ Wash chholar dal in water.

- ♪ Pressure cook 1 cup dal with 2–3 cups of water, turmeric and little salt for 6–7 minutes after steam has built up in the cooker (say about 10–12 minutes overall). The lentils should be soft and cooked but remain separate by this time. If they have not reached this stage, you need to cook more.

- ♪ Heat the oil and ghee in a kadhai or in a soup pot.

- ♪ Temper the oil with the whole spices listed under tempering. Add a pinch of hing/asafoetida.

- ♪ When the spices pop, add very finely chopped onion and minced garlic.
- ♪ Fry till onion is slightly brown at the edges, for about 3 minutes.
- ♪ Add the pureed tomato and minced ginger to the kadhai and fry till the oil separates from the masala. This should take around 4–5 minutes. Increase onion and chilli if you want a spicier version.
- ♪ Drain water from the cooked dal. Reserve the dal water for later use. Add the cooked dal gradually to the kadhai and fry the dal for 4–5 minutes. Add the red chilli powder.
- ♪ Add the reserved dal water along with 1 cup more of water. Add salt to taste. Bengali dals are a little on the sweet side, so add sugar.
- ♪ Let the dal come to a boil. Add a little more water if you think the dal is too thick for you.
- ♪ Add ghee if you have not used ghee in the cooking process. Taste and adjust for seasoning. Serve with white rice or hot puffed luchis.

While this chholar dal has garlic, the traditional chholar dal is shuddh niramish, garnished with raisins and fried pieces of coconut. Chholar dal narkel diye is a very popular Bengali dish and is a fixed item on the menu during wedding feasts or Durga Pujo bhog, the food offered to the goddess after prayers. It is mostly cooked on special occasions and those range from the only-daughter's-getting-the-visa-day to the only-son's-homecoming-day. It is usually not an everyday dal though you could have it so if you wanted to.

The recipes for both these dals are similar but the traditional chholar dal does not have onion, garlic or tomatoes. Instead, golden raisins are added to the simmering dal and it is garnished with fried pieces of coconut.

KALAI'ER DAL
White urad dal cooked the Bong way

Kalai'er dal is made of split white urad dal, is very typically Bengali and also a favourite in many Bengali homes. Kalai'er dal with aloo posto or aloo seddho (mashed potatoes with a dash of mustard oil) is the best thing that can happen to you during a lulled summer afternoon lunch. If I think of an Indian summer I think of this dal and aloo seddho as much as I think of mangoes like himsagar and lyangra. Strange are the thoughts of the human mind. Flavoured with ada-mouri bata (a paste of ginger and fennel seeds) this sweet smelling dal can take on two different avatars.

If you do not roast the urad dal before cooking, it tends to get a bit slimy. Many people do not like the slippery texture though personally, I love it.

If you dry roast the dal before you cook, the slimy texture goes and you get the flavourful dal without the slippery feeling.

This dal is best enjoyed with white rice. In a Bengali home, it is typically served with aloo posto or aloo seddho during a quiet lunch for the family.

1	cup split white urad dal	1"	ginger piece
4–5	green chillies		Salt to taste
¼	tsp hing/asafoetida	¼	tsp sugar
2	tsp fennel seeds/mouri	1	tbsp vegetable oil

- Grind the fennel seeds and ginger with a splash of water to make a paste of ada-mouri bata (a wet paste of ginger and fennel seeds).

- Dry roast the urad dal till you get a fine roasted smell and about 50 per cent of the lentils turn a light brown. This will take around 5 minutes. Wash the roasted dal lightly. If you do not want to roast it, you can skip this step.

- Pressure cook the urad dal with almost two times the water. When it's cooked, lightly mix it with a whisk. Do not mash it up. It may take 5–6 minutes to get done in the cooker after the pressure builds up.

- Heat the oil in a kadhai. Add the slit green chillies and the hing.

- Add the ada-mouri bata. Fry the paste for about 2–3 minutes at medium heat and when you get the sweet smell of the masala, add the dal. Fry the dal for a couple of minutes.

- Add about 1 cup water and salt and let it cook.

- This is not a very thick dal so add 1 cup more water if needed.

- Enjoy it with white rice, aloo posto and some bhaja (fried veggie fritters). Kalai'er dal is also very tasty with a side of aloo seddho.

Musur'ir Dal on a Jet Plane

Every summer we (i.e., the family) try to wrangle a week's vacation in the busy calendar. The girls have two months off. According to the US academic calendar, 'school off' means really, truly 'off'. Summer vacation does not involve pages of writing and decimals.

It is a blissful life. For them, that is. Parents, on the other hand, have to run around like headless chickens, fixing up summer camp, play-dates and applying for a week's worth of vacation. Flight ticket prices soar with the mercury and to get anything even close to a habitable shack on the Atlantic coast is a miracle. Of course, given my upbringing, I think it is frivolous.

Why can't summer be unplanned, like it used to? Most summer vacations, all my mother did was let me loose in my grandmother's house. She had it easy and I didn't end up in a psychiatric ward. Instead, the summers of my childhood have merged into one another, blending into one happy, colourful blob. If I furrow my brows and concentrate, I see long, hot days broken by the guttural humming of the ceiling fan, windows shut tight even before noon, cool damp floors, mangoes ripening in sacks in the darkness beneath grandfather's master bed and tall glasses of Rasna tinkling with ice. Meals in those summer days were simple. Dull green lauki or jhinge, a pale watery musurir dal and a light fish curry with fragrant white gobindobhog rice was the staple. My grandmother would often make tok'er dal with firm green mangoes on those sweltering hot afternoons, the sour mangoes favoured for their cooling effect in the heat.

My girls would brand that summer 'b-o-r-i-n-g'. So in the quest for excitement, we plan vacations and buy happiness.

To tell you the truth, on a holiday that involves two kids, I am usually comfortable with two-hour road trips. In my travel advisory, trips involving flight and restricted luggage are solely taken for the purpose of going to India. It therefore came as a surprise when the H-man decided on a trans-Atlantic Denmark trip in the name of vacation and the girls shouted 'Yay!' I needed smelling salts.

This is how we landed up at Copenhagen airport two

summers ago, early in the morning. 5:55 a.m., to be precise. That is not a time I like to find myself anywhere, forget airports. There we were with two kids and eight pieces of luggage, departing after a week's worth of holidaying in the Danish countryside. A few hundred people were ahead of us and 'Københavns Lufthavn' looked very similar to Howrah Station, albeit cleaner.

Except for size 0, pretty young girls with single Gucci bags, everyone had multiple Samsonites. I threw a triumphant look at the H-man. After all, he is the one with the 'travel light' mantra. He had thrown up all kinds of resistance to my need to pack a small world.

'Why do you need to carry three pairs of shoes for only six days?'

'Box of Cheerios? Nutella? Are you crazy? Do you realize we are not going camping?'

He did not understand my need to carry all the above and a small bottle of dishwashing liquid for a six day trip to a civilized country. In fact, he wasn't too happy with all the other people and their luggage either. That made sense because when the large family ahead of us finally checked in their fifth skateboard and gathered their boarding passes, there were only fifteen minutes left for departure.

With a backpack weighing 35lb on my right shoulder, a diaper bag hanging from my left and my handbag around my neck, I geared up for a sprint. The seven year old was swift. The little one, sitting on her Dad's shoulders, was actually enjoying the early morning exercise. Me, I panted and puffed and kept reminding myself of the long forgotten gym membership. I would sign up for the next NYC marathon, I promised myself.

The stocky security officials delayed me further by enquiring about the various liquids that I had stuffed in the diaper bag. I hyperventilated. By the time they let me go with my bodywash and obnoxious beeping undergarment (and it wasn't even a chastity belt that I was wearing), Iceland Air was making its last call.

And then at 37,000 feet, when they served me a ham and cheese sandwich in a cling wrap with a sad lettuce leaf, my frazzled nerves finally snapped. Ignoring the pathetic sandwich, I fished a Tupperware box from my bottomless sling bag. I opened the lid and took a deep whiff of rice mixed with a pale yellow masoor dal, a meal which I had cooked in the hotel microwave that morning. It was cold but delicious. The H-man raised an eyebrow and silently asked for his share. He didn't dare to ask any stupid questions like 'Why do you need masoor dal on a jet plane?'

After a week of delicious Thai food, refreshing Greek fare, mustardy hot dogs and sad-creamy Indian butter chickens, all a Bengali wants is some pale, light with a hint of lime musuri'r dal and fluffy white rice. I would have given anything for it, even my ticket on a jet plane.

Bangali Musuri'r Dal
The red masoor dal

This is the dal my family looks forward to when we are down, depressed, tired, anxious, worried or hard-pressed for time.

When we have travelled across continents, missed flights, handled crying babies, lived on tasteless airline food, lost luggage and come home bearing sweet memories of grandparents, aunts and cousins, this is the dal we cook.

We make it quickly (there's no way you can lengthen the process anyway), eat it with white rice and aloo seddho with green chillies and lemon on the side and bask in its warmth, slowly forgetting the gloom that had shrouded us.

If I am in a good mood and do not need all the carbs to lift my spirit, I have this dal as a soup and feel the same contentment.

This dal is like Zen. If you have a bowlful of this you will never, ever need a therapist or a yoga teacher or a tight rope walker or a snake charmer. You will never need anything more.

1 cup masoor dal/split red lentils washed thoroughly	**For garnish:**
1 medium sized red onion, sliced in thin long slices	4 tsp fresh lime juice
	3–4 sprigs coriander leaves
1 firm red tomato, chopped fine	Salt to taste
2–3 finely chopped green chillies	½ tsp sugar
For tempering:	½ tsp turmeric powder
1 tsp paanch-phoron	2 tsp mustard oil (or use vegetable oil)

- Pressure cook the masoor dal with 2 and ½ cups of water and turmeric powder. Once it is cooked mix it well with a whisk. The time taken to cook depends on your cooker. I use a Futura which needs 3 minutes after the full steam build-up.

- Heat oil and temper with Paanch-phoron.

- Add the finely sliced onions and fry till they turn pink. Add the chopped green chillies. Add the chopped tomatoes and cook till they become a fine pulp.

- Add the previously cooked dal and mix well. Add salt, sugar and about 3–4 cups of water. If you feel you need to add more water, do so. Cook till you hear a bubbling sound. Remember to stir infrequently during this process. Continue to cook till the thickness of the dal is according to your liking.

ঌ Garnish with chopped coriander leaves and lime juice.

Note: With simple variations of phoron you can make a different dal.

Try a phoron or tempering of kalo jeera (nigella seeds) and kancha lonka (green chillies). Skip the onions to get the same dal in a new avatar. Another variation is a tempering with the highly esteemed radhuni and a pinch of hing. To make a sour tauker dal, cook dal with chunks of green mango and then temper the dal with mustard seeds and dry red chilli and skip the onion and tomato.

The Garam Masala Tales

Bengali garam masala is actually a very simple mix of four spices: cloves, cardamom, cinnamon and bay leaves. These are often used whole as phoron to temper and spice the oil used for cooking. My mother would sun these spices and use our stainless steel Bajaj mixer to make a dry powder. She would then store it as a guro garam mashla, garam masala powder.

I go a step further and put more stuff in my garam masala powder. I also dry roast the spices instead of just sunning them, which is the norm. The Bengali version does not usually have red chilli or mace which I add.

Lightly dry roast or warm in the sun the following whole spices: 20 green cardamom, 10 clove, a 2 inch stick of cinnamon, 3–4 dry red chilli for the slightest heat, 2–3 small barks of mace and a small bay leaf. You can substitute red chilli with black peppercorn.

Grind them to a fine powder in your coffee grinder. Store in an air-tight container for future use.

Office romances. Unrequited love. Long distance relationships. All of this needs the support structure of lemon-flavoured dal, butter-laden creamy gravies and long grain basmati cooked in loads of dalda with chicken and brown fried onions. Trust me on that.

That is what Bombay (where I first started my independent life), a limited budget and friends who share a love for food taught me. When I think of Bombay, I don't think of the monsoon, SRK or Marine Drive. Instead, I think of mornings at the beautiful, terraced office cafeteria – the prime reason for my acceptance of that job.

After all, I had given up perfectly good job offers because the offering companies had spartan vegetarian menus. My standard request at campus interviews was 'Can I get a sample of the weekly menu, sir?' No wonder I had been elated when I clinched this job in Bombay.

Mornings there always remind me of my friend M and the cafeteria. 'Veg or Egg,' M ponders, her hair in a messy plait, her t-shirt and jeans in a state of permanent dishevelment. The svelte Mumbai girls in their designer jeans snigger at us. They probably survive on air to look like that. We, the 'khata-pita' big Bong crowd, gather around, our eyes squinting at the menu hastily scrawled on the whiteboard, mulling over the consequences our decisions can have.

Tough life choices. Two slices of bleached white bread slapped together with some Amul butter, slices of cold boiled egg, sagging tomatoes and slivers of cucumber demand as much attention as the new gel-haired intern smelling of drugstore aftershave.

If you must know, I was raised by strict Bengali parents. There is no other kind, by the way. In the nineties, I wore thick black-rimmed glasses from Himalaya Opticals because I wanted to look antel aka intellectual. My salwar-kameez were tailormade in north Calcutta by a guy whose idea of fine dressing ended with *Mughal-e-Azam*. I had been brought up to believe 'shiny black hair' meant a head doused with gallons of coconut oil and mustard oil solved the world's problems. There was hardly anything going for me. Of course the gel-haired paid me little attention. Instead I spent my mornings standing with my motley group, food coupon in hand, gravely discussing the merits of boiled eggs over cucumber. That made me relatively happy, buoyant and even optimistic about my future.

If the muhurtam seemed right, I took my optimism further and asked the bhaiyya manning the cafeteria 'Lunch mein kya hai? What's for lunch?'

On days when he said 'Biryani', the day moved swiftly until noon struck. The lunch would settle heavy in my belly and soon my eyes would glaze, struggling just to keep staring at the computer. And at exactly three in the afternoon, when M popped her head over the cubicle to announce 'Tea?', it sounded better than any well-meaning appraisal.

On this cue, I would collect my tea in a styrofoam cup, gather my fellow Bongs and troop outside to the farsaan store next to the office building.

This was the suburbs of Mumbai in the nineties and farsaan store owners were mustachioed and bespectacled friendly folk who would insist on ghee laden, warm yellow besan laddoos and vada pav. These were a delicacy then unknown to our Bengali palate and as much as we complained that nothing could compare to hot kathi egg roll or phuchka by New Empire, every afternoon we diligently walked out in single file, down four stories, past the security guards, and onto the dusty streets to the farsaan store next door.

Considering this routine, it is inevitable that Mumbai reminds me of warm cups of insipid vending machine tea spiked with sunny balls of vada and soft pav, pudgy and white like the palms of a baby fed on ghee and butter.

Weekend eating was a lot more complicated though. Our salary was meagre and many a dull Saturday would find my flatmate and me hunched over a single plate of chhole bhature at Sukh Sagar.

Once a month however, the situation got better. The sun sparkled, birds broke into song, rainbows in acrylic colours formed a perfect arc and harps played in the clouds. Ta-da. Payday was here. And it wasn't any aisa-waisa payday. Nope. It was a day which demanded that we auto-train-bus-walk all the way from Borivali to Nariman Point to collect the money from the hallowed interiors of a multinational bank.

The only comforting thing about that journey was the thick wad of notes at the end of the rainbow and the food that we would eat along the way.

The food trail would begin at Churchgate station with the Frankie's roll. Armed with that and a muddy bottle of masala milk from the Arrey milk booth, we would walk to Nariman Point.

The soiled wad of notes from the bank would then be spent on oil-drenched hakka noodles from the Chinese thelawalas, on the salty windswept biryani redolent with spices and mint near Gateway of India and on umpteen buttery pav-bhaji stalls in between.

On days when we were in serious need of a sugar fix, we would go all the way to Malad where hearsay had it that the sweetest, thickest rabri was made by a local halwai. The place was close to the station, in a crowded galli where kids in dusty clothes played cricket right in the midst of honking autos.

The halwai sat outside the store behind a huge, wide-mouthed kadhai, stirring bubbling white milk with a long handled ladle. The milk frothed and rippled, forming a thin, cloth-like layer on the surface. He would then pull this layer aside and coax the milk to thicken and reduce some more. Thick, hot air hung around him. His forehead shone in the afternoon sun and it was obvious he had been doing this for hours. By then the milk would have taken on a creamy shade and the sweet fragrance was enough to attract people and flies alike. He ladled the warm rabri into small earthenware pots called kulhar which we then ate with tiny wooden spoons, seated on the bench outside.

We ate junk. We ate cheap. And while my mom spent Sunday afternoons scouring the matrimony columns of *Anandabazar Patrika*, we crisscrossed Mumbai's suburban lines just to eat and taste different foods. One factor motivating us, of course, was the prospect of getting away from cooking at home. Cooking was such a chore. Who did that? We were new age modern women after all.

Somewhere down the line our love for greasy bhaturas and engine oil chicken bhartas took a beating. The weekend Bengali dinner at an aunt's home in Kandivali seemed far more attractive. The Sunday the Bengali guys from work invited us to a homecooked murgir jhol scarlet with red chillies and bobbing with buttery potatoes, my roommate and I bought packets of garam masala, jeera powder, a new kadhai and walked back home with a renewed interest in cooking for ourselves

I discovered small pleasures in standing by the kitchen window, chopping onions or green chillies and looking out at the small sliver of blue sky that Mumbai high-rises offered. The twice weekly STD calls back home from the phone booth across the street were gradually being peppered with more recipes than I had ever asked for. Calls often got longer as Ma frantically tried to explain the visual difference between chana dal and arhar dal while a serpentine queue formed outside the booth door. My roommate and I graduated from dal to egg curry and even cauliflower curry during the one year that I stayed there.

Armed with our newly acquired skills, we invited all of the twenty Bengalis we knew in the office over for a Sunday lunch.

The menu was simple. All the four items we knew were on it: rice, dal, egg curry and the phulkopir dalna I had recently learnt over the telephone. My roomie wasn't too sure about it. I oozed confidence. Hah, what was a cauliflower in the hands of an excellent cook like yours truly?

We did not have a refrigerator, so on that Sunday morning we started our preparation by procuring produce. Fresh, local, organic – everything was available just across the busy main street. One cauliflower, one kg potatoes, two dozen eggs, onions, green chillies, tomato, coriander leaves. The shopping bag was loaded. By the time we returned, dusty, hot and tired, it was late morning.

My roommate was to cook the egg curry; I was doing dal and phulkopir dalna. We had only one single burner gas and we were cooking quite a large amount of food. By the time we were done with the egg curry and rice, the guests had arrived. We decided to chuck the dal and go straight for the phulkopir dalna. The cauliflower florets had already been cut and were soaking lazily in a big bowl of water.

I fired up the big kadhai and splashed a good deal of oil in it. Meanwhile, some of the friends had moved over to the kitchen as there was little place to wander in the one-roomed apartment. I appeared nonchalant in spite of the audience, totally at ease. I even tried conducting some small-talk while waiting for the oil to heat up.

'You know Shilpa on the fifth floor in the Sys Admin group? Do you know she has something going on with the HR guy?' The oil heated up, waiting for me while I analyzed Shilpa and her HR guy.

At this point a friend shrieked, 'Smoke, smoke… behind you!'

I turned my head. Smoke was rising furiously from the aluminium kadhai.

'Oh, it is all nicely heated up. Let me put in the phulkopi,' My voice was cool, calm and collected. I wanted to do a female Sanjeev Kapoor. I was the chef extraordinaire, after all.

With that I dunked the entire bowl of phulkopi, water et al, into the kadhai. Hisss. The hot oil splashed angrily and blisters blossomed on my skin. I was terrified, my friends were terrified, the lesser known friends who had come over to break bread with us on a lovely Sunday afternoon were scarred forever and never returned.

Later in the afternoon, we ate rice, egg curry and pickle and soothed pain with yellow tubes of Burnol.

For a long time after that, I dunked my cauliflower florets in oil by taking aim from a distance. Cooking needed respect and care. I had learned my lesson.

By God!
Bongs Also Eat Veggies!

Years ago, we ate vegetables according to season. Spring, summer, monsoon, autumn, winter... we waited for vegetables to grow and then ate what was harvested in those months. Cooked with seasonal vegetables, lentils, vadis and spices, a full Bengali vegetarian meal was not just a meal, it was an event.

Recently I achieved the status of Bong mashimadom. I dispense Bryonia 30, advice on handling toddler tantrums and recipes of daler bora like a pro. I update my Facebook status with questions like 'What is THE Bengali vegetarian dish you would take for a potluck?'.

'Aloor dom,' says one.

'Kaanchkolar kofta with green plantain. Do you have the recipe on your blog?' quips another.

'Your begun bhaja is a big hit with my American friends,' says a twenty-something who 'likes' my status.

I don't tell them that unlike my training with dal, I didn't learn to cook any fancy Bengali vegetables other than a phulkopir dalna until I came to the United States. And the cauliflower curry was not even that fancy.

A decade ago, I did not believe in Bong vegetables. If I had to be an herbivore, malai kofta or shredded cabbage in my Schezwan noodles was the way to go. 'Mochar ghonto', 'dhokar dalna', 'daler bora' uttered in a single sentence phased me out. I was in no rush to attain the hallowed status of the Bengali mashima. A life of fame awaited me and 'chorchori' did not feature there – that was how I assured myself.

These days my blog readers send me mails asking for recipes of chapor ghonto made with complex vegetables. Clearly I have come a long way. But really, chapor ghonto? That's pushing it.

On my first flight to the US, a year after my marriage, I carried two suitcases. One of them was a VIP Elanza, deep navy grey with handsome ebony number locking snaps. My Baba, the packer in the family, had packed it on a sweaty July afternoon, sitting cross-legged on the floor of our Kolkata apartment. It must have been difficult for him, given that he was a worrier, his daughter was travelling continents and he had a lot of stuff to pack. But he had managed to fit in a Futura pressure cooker, a Prestige non-stick kadhai, a shanrashi, a tea sieve and some La Opala bowls from my wedding gifts. He had also filled the void with jars of Jharna ghee wrapped in several layers of dupatta, two plastic bottles of Dhara shorsher tel, packets of fragrant gobindobhog rice fit for the consumption of Lord Krishna, orange packets of mukhorochak 'tok-jhaal-mishti' chanachur and two copies of Bela De cookbooks written in Bangla.

Not to be outdone, my Ma had arranged several packets of dusky black cumin seeds, coriander seeds the colour of dried summer grass, tiny white poppy seeds and black mustard seeds in a shoe box. I don't know if they expected me to cook up a storm in a foreign country or if this was a way for them to pack a slice of home on my journey. But that is how I took flight across continents, armed with a suitcase full of spices.

I had heard enough horror stories to be scared stiff at the immigration counter in JFK. I had been regaled with tales of cousins who had to dump a kilo of fresh patol because the INS did not allow food items. The story about my aunt's second brother who was handcuffed and paroled because he was carrying a packet of poppy seeds for his daughter-in-law was a family legend. My aunt in Mumbai had her own stories of how she had done reiki or some such thing and thus fooled the INS officers. My extended family's sole purpose of travel seemed to be to transport edibles unbeknownst to customs officials.

By the time my flight landed, I had made up my mind. If the officers stopped me, I would give up the mango sondesh that my Ma had sent for her son-in-law. The spices would remain with me. Always.

Surprisingly, most of the spices sat in that suitcase for a long time; except for the pressure cooker and the tea sieve, I found no immediate use for anything. By the time the Elanza was unpacked, its silky inseams bore an oily patch from where the ghee had leaked, and yet I did not venture into the unknown where Bengali food was concerned.

By now I had been in holy matrimony for about a year and knew the H-man well enough not to try to impress him, at least not with my cooking. He was a non-fussy eater but a fastidious cook, a fact I hadn't got a whiff of in all the four years we had known each other. Our relationship had blossomed – if 'blossom' is a word applicable to anything that involves the H-man – over food. But never did I realize that when he said 'golden fried onions', he meant a particular shade in the Asian paints colour chart. For me it could mean anything between the stages when onions had turned pink to a step before they burnt.

Only a couple of months into our marriage, when we were still living in the very cosmopolitan Bangalore, one evening at dinner, he dismissed my egg curry. 'This is not an egg curry,' he declared after a month of gulping down the same dish. 'This is a mere amalgamation of eggs, onion, potatoes, turmeric and water.' I was outraged. This was not just any egg curry. It was one that I had painstakingly built on in my singleton Mumbai life and was almost proud of.

Every day for one whole month I had cooked it repeatedly from memory and this was what it led to? Even before the mehendi stains had washed off my hands, my marriage had shattered. Well, almost. The H-man clearly did not see it from my perspective. He believed in being honest. I guess he deduced even if it cost a marriage it would at least result in a better egg curry.

So when I flared, raised a mini-war and handed over dinner duties to him, he actually gladly took it up. He was relieved; and watching him surreptitiously, I learned the true meaning of 'fry till oil separates from masala'. To my utter shock, it wasn't just a turn of phrase like 'spill the beans' or 'bust your chops' as I had assumed, but was a miracle where the oil really separated from the mix of spices.

Once in the US, GRE, university applications and complex control theory made sure that I did not invest too much time in cooking. In our charming apartment with broad maple leaves hanging over the verandah there were newer obstacles in my culinary path. The very modern kitchen had a smoke alarm which broke the silence of an otherwise eerily quiet neighbourhood with every begun bhaja I fried and the nice Irish lady who lived upstairs (and cooked a pungent cabbage stew on Fridays) sneezed violently every time I tempered smoking hot mustard oil with dry red chillies.

I played safe and in those early days I did not cook anything beyond a simple dal, rice and egg curry tempered with fragrant paanch-phoron. The egg curry had improved and now had a pretty red colour with a slick layer of oil floating on top. At night we would sit on the wooden floor of our single bedroom apartment, spread out centre folds from the *New York Times* on the floor and serve ourselves straight from the pot on plain white ceramic plates – hand-me-downs from the H-man's kind colleague. If we were careful we could keep the paper for use again the next day.

On weekends, the H-man made his trademark chicken curry which we will talk about later.

Thai Tom Yum soup perfumed with lime leaves, sticky Kung Pao chicken in cardboard boxes from the Chinese takeout, thin crust pizzas and juicy hot dogs with mustard, relish and ketchup from tiny sachets – this is how we explored the new country on weekdays. In extreme cases I would make Thai red curry with flavours of fresh green basil and store-bought red curry paste or cook a chilli chicken browned with soy sauce and coated with cornflour. And on snowy days, when the heart craved home, we would make shingaras, triangular crisp packets of flaky dough filled with spiced potatoes and peas that refused to stand on their fat bottoms and would instead fall.

Vegetables – Bengali vegetables – did not feature on our menu.

And then one fine day we were invited to a Bong party – an evening of food and only food cooked by a very generous Bengali hostess. The invitation had a timbre of mystery as we did not really know the Bengali family who accosted us at Durga Pujo and insisted that we visit them. 'You have to come', the gentleman had said. His wife, a lady with heavy gold adornments, had nodded along smilingly. It being a Bong party and all, we did not refuse. Till then we had been unaware of such parties. Most of our friends led dull, unshaven lives where a party at home involved rice and chicken cooked together in a pressure cooker and lots of drinks.

That this evening was to turn out different was evident when we entered the host's home. It was a chilly October evening. Fairy lights twinkled on the front porch and carved Halloween pumpkins bared their teeth by the door. Through the frosted glass of the front door we caught a glimpse of fine, creamy tussars and animated hands weighed down with gold. Feeling very inadequate in our jeans and t-shirts, we were ushered with much warmth into a home that smelled of fragrant roasted cumin and rich zafran laced with the sweet scent of kewra water. The gracious hostess handed us our appetizer plates. They carried vegetable chop shaped like a plump side pillow with a sprinkle of beet noon and a yellow ghugni, chickpeas garnished liberally with chopped green coriander and onion. One bite of that ethereal chop and all I could do was wait impatiently for dinner.

That night, the food-laden rosewood table was beyond my wildest dreams. There were several of everything. Two kinds of dal, four different vegetable dishes, two kinds of fish preparation and then a shrimp, a mutton curry and a chicken kosha, a pineapple chutney and a tomato one, followed by two different kinds of dessert. It was clear that the hostess had been up since an ungodly hour, cooking for fifty people, food that would have served a wedding feast. The amazing thing was that all the dishes on the table had a Bengali past. There was shorshe begun, where tender fried slices of eggplant were soaked in a silky yellow mustard gravy and a kaanchkolar kofta curry with koftas of green plantains and potatoes bobbing in a gravy of onion and tomatoes. There was a cauliflower roast just like my mother's, heady with the scent of cinnamon, and a paanch-mishali, a mix of five different vegetables garnished with crumbs of fried brown vadi.

My taste buds woke up with a jolt. The food was so familiar and so good that it hurt. Amidst the rustle of the Dhakai sarees and the discussions about the latest acquisitions of gold on Kolkata trips, I was transported home.

I had attained moksha.

In this perfect state of being, while I was intently trying to debone the tricky koi maachh on my paper plate, the host — in his mid-fifties with a salt-and-pepper goatee — sat down beside me, wine glass in hand.

'So how is the PhD coming along?' he asked.

PhD? Me? I almost choked on the koi fish bone. Wasn't toiling at my Masters hard enough? What was he, my dad's secret spy?

'Professor Puri is a master in organic chemistry', he continued. 'He was actually praising your recent paper on nano-porous materials the other day'.

This was news to me. First, I had not the least idea who Professor Puri was, however great a master he might be. Second, I had never even heard of nano-porous materials, forget written any paper on them. Organic Chemistry was never my forte.

'What is a nano-porous material?' I asked, licking the last traces of the pineapple chutney from my fingers.

My host looked doubtful. He scratched his goatee. 'Aren't you Sudipta, working under Professor Puri?' he finally asked.

I earnestly wanted to be if that would give the poor man any solace, but better sense prevailed. 'I would love to be, but no, I am a very different person,' I said. He was bewildered. Looking around at the H-man, he said 'Then this young person must be the one. Maybe the Professor meant Sudipto.'

The H-man had as good an idea about Puri the Professor as I did. I could see the desperate look in his eyes. A sumptuous dessert of lyangcha and bhapa doi was still to be had. It seemed futile to let go of it just because we had not written a paper on some porous stuff. Chewing on a fat marrowed bone, the H-man contemplated our next move. Fortuitously, our host took his silence as acquiescence and didn't bother us any further.

We left soon after dessert, avoiding any further academic discussion.

I was so deluged with nostalgia at this meal that soon after, I spent an evening and better part of the night trying to make posto bata, grinding poppy seeds in the mortar that I had got from a Chinese store. Thak, thak, thak. I patiently pounded, sitting on the wooden floor of my living room till one in the night. The sound bothered the upstairs Irish neighbour so much that we got a warning notice of eviction the next day.

It turned out I was the only idiot who had no clue about the coffee grinder that every Indian in the US has put to use to grind dry spices.

I must admit here that we never invited the couple in return to our home. Honestly we did not have the courage even to attempt to match their banquet with our limited culinary skills and mismatched crockery. We never found out who Professor Puri was either.

Instead, we went to Wal-Mart and after much deliberation bought a matching set of Corelle plates and bowls with a pattern of leafy green twirls all around. That and small glass spice jars on a rotating wooden base. Our life in spice had just begun.

After my daughter was born, I realized the importance of the social fabric that formed a backdrop to our lives and the role food played in it. In between diaper changes, breastfeeding and sleepless nights, I also learned to entertain, to be the Bengali hostess, to cook for a child's birthday party as only a Bengali would.

Around this time, most of my 'culinary-da-expert' friends were actually drifting away from homecooking and getting into flying rockets or bungee jumping. Those who had made the perfect spongy rosogollas at home were now learning to change tyres. Duck pate in foie gras and batter-fried quail was in. Homecooking was passé. I was clearly late in the game. But that did not bother me. For me this was an exciting and adventure-filled journey.

My quest to broaden my horizons and expand my repertoire of Bengali recipes took me out of my comfort zone. I asked around. I picked up the helpful suggestion of grinding mustard seeds with salt and green chilli to avoid bitterness. When a new friend made a shorshe dharosh whose raunchy taste lingered on my tongue, I unabashedly asked her for the recipe. I called Ma and asked her about her phulkopir roast. I translated her helpful hints of 'a pinch of garam masala and a lot of ginger' into what I thought was needed in the recipe. I clipped recipes from *Sananda* on my annual Kolkata visits and, much later, asked people for recipes on Facebook.

And then I started a food blog.

SHORSHE DHAROSH
Okra in mustard sauce

Bengalis tend to eat a lot of shorshe or mustard and will douse everything on earth in this sauce. Many vegetables, like eggplant and okra, taste wonderful when cooked in mustard sauce. Though eggplant cooked with mustard is more common; here I have cooked tender baby okra in a similar sauce. If you prefer eggplant, follow the same recipe but use eggplant instead of okra.

Serve this dish with fluffy white rice and eat with your fingers to best enjoy the taste of mustard.

18–20 bhindi/okra

To make mustard paste:
- 1 tbsp mustard seeds
- ½ tbsp posto/poppy seeds
- 2 tbsp fresh grated coconut (optional)
- 1 tbsp yoghurt
- 1 tbsp water
- 4 green chillies
- Salt to taste

- 1 tbsp kasundi. If you do not have kasundi, double your mustard paste by using 2 tbsp mustard and 1 tbsp poppy seeds.

For tempering:
- ¼ tsp nigella seeds
- ½ tsp turmeric powder

Salt to taste
Sugar to taste (optional)
- 2 tbsp mustard oil

♪ Wash the okra and then pat dry. Chop off the head and tail after drying.

♪ Soak mustard and poppy seeds in water for 20 minutes and then make a mustard paste with all ingredients listed under 'mustard paste'. The paste should be smooth. If more water is needed add a small quantity. Instead of the paste you can also use the readymade mustard powder.

Note: If the pungency of the mustard is too much for you, you can sieve the mustard paste and use the mustardy water, but then you need more of the paste to make enough liquid.

♪ Heat 1 tbsp oil in a shallow frying pan. Sauté the okra with a sprinkle of turmeric at medium heat. Cover and sauté for about 4 minutes till okra is lightly fried but not fully cooked. Sprinkle salt and remove and keep aside.

♪ Heat another tbsp oil. Temper the oil with nigella seeds. When the seeds start sputtering, lower the heat and add the mustard paste. Cook the paste for a minute at low-medium heat. Add the kasundi. Then add the lightly fried okra. Add ¼ tsp turmeric powder. Raise the heat and toss everything well together for one more minute.

♪ Now add 4–5 tbsp water and salt to taste and cover the pan. If you have added kasundi be careful with the salt. Let the okra cook in the mustard sauce. If needed add a little more water. The tender okra will cook fast and will be done in about 5–6 minutes. Remove the cover and check. The sauce will be thick and clinging to the okra. Add a little sugar and mix nicely. Drizzle a tsp mustard oil and serve hot. Tastes best with white rice.

Begun bhaja – a quick and easy party favourite

Chop a good quality eggplant in thick rounds or half moon shapes.

Wash well, pat dry and smear with a little turmeric and salt. Set aside for 10–15 minutes.

Heat mustard oil to smoking.

Slide the eggplant slices gently into the hot oil and shallow fry till golden. Take out with a slotted spoon and drain on a kitchen towel.

The Fancy Bengali Vegetarian

When I started my blog some years ago, I had no set plan for it. Cook, eat, blog — that was the general idea. At the least I had expected to become the self-appointed flag bearer of Bengali cuisine. However, I was soon going around protesting myths such as 'Bengali cuisine is time-consuming and involves a complex blend of spices' and refuting discussions which whined 'Despite its uniqueness, Bengali food failed to grow beyond connoisseurs. Traditional Bengali cuisine is gradually becoming a dying art'. Clearly my passion was growing in leaps and bounds. Whether that was a good thing or a bad thing was undecided.

But honestly, if you can ignore the purists, Bengali food is not all that complex. Subtle, flitting, unobtrusive like a handful of fresh ricotta? Yes. Complex? No. A mix of spices here, a small pinch of cumin-coriander there, a dash of mustard oil as a secret ingredient and voila! You have a subtly spiced dish with the undisguised taste of all the vegetables in full flavour. You don't always have to do it right and you can make your bhapa ilish in the oven or even the microwave, but the basic thing is you can still fit it in a day when your child has to practise her Rabindrasangeet. That, I think, is important.

I get my fair share of puritan comments on the blog which declare my cabbage sabzi is not authentic or that I am alienating Bengali traditions by making my bhapa doi in the oven. I dismiss them with a grumpy 'Hrrmpf' and go about my mission of popularizing Bengali Food.

So in this new role I had found an opportunity to win glory for my much-loved Bengali food — to present my cuisine on a global platform. I had ruminated on it so much that now only two days were left and I was yet to do something concrete about it.

You see, every year before Thanksgiving and around Diwali we have a multi-cultural lunch at work. It is the American boss's brilliant idea to bring otherwise disgruntled employees, hacking away at the keyboard, to bond over falafel and chicken tikka masala. He has good intentions. I am not sure how much bonding happens but so far no one has complained about the falafel or the tikka. One time there was an issue with the rosogolla I had taken. The syrup had dripped down the sleeves of some 'high up in the food chain' guy's dress shirt and there was much scoffing and annoyance followed by a chain of serious e-mails.

We have since been asked to describe the dish and correct procedure of eating it before the event. But that is what I had done in the very first place! I had said very clearly that you hold the rosogolla between your thumb and index finger and then pop it in your mouth at one go. Only, I had forgotten to mention the right amount of pressure the fingers should apply.

So this lunch thing was two days away and I wasn't sure what to bring. The other Indian from the north had already claimed chhole. His wife was an authority on butter paneer, navratan korma and kali dal, so I couldn't touch those with a barge pole. There was also the fact that I wanted to bring a vegetarian dish that represented Bengal and I had no clue what fit the bill.

The assertion that Bengali cuisine is understated and not really that popular outside Bengal is not totally false. Bengali vegetable dishes usually need a certain finesse to get the clean flavour with the minimum of spices, a fact which makes it hard to re-create them en masse. I could say it is like French cuisine, served in small portions over multiple courses, but there is no restaurant on 64th Street, Manhattan to prove it. Even if you ignore the global West, most Indians outside of Bengal think Bengali food is all about fish and sweets. That Bongs eat veggies is a mystery to many.

As I randomly asked around for suggestions, the south Indian girl from HR looked at me quizzically and said, 'Really, you guys have different vegetable dishes? I thought Bengalis only ate fish and rosogolla. You bring rosogolla for dessert'.

I glared back and said, 'Yeah, we eat fish and sweets and then just keep repeating the pattern until we are full or in a state of malnutrition.' The joke was lost on her.

The gora network guy said, 'Get paneer tikka. I love the paneer tikka at Taj Mahal.' I ignored him. What did he know? The poor guy hadn't even heard of Shah Jahan.

I was in a dilemma. I searched high and low and of course there were a variety of Bengali vegetarian dishes but I wasn't sure which one would be a crowd pleaser at a potluck. There was shukto, the highbrow of Bengali cuisine. But that was hard to explain to palates assaulted by layers of cream in the name of Indian food. Shukto needed time to get used to and only then could be loved. That wasn't going to happen when paired with dim-sum and butter naan.

Then there was the paanch-mishali or the chorchori. Again, they needed an ambience, an awareness of Ray, a whiff of Tagore's *Shesher Kobita* and at least some musuri'r dal and rice to go along with it.

I could have settled on dhokar dalna and raised the bar high but that would mean too much work and I wasn't going to make a spiced lentil-cake curry for an office party that had no promise of a bonus afterwards.

I was clearly hyperventilating now over the single dish that would be the El Dorado of Bong vegetarianism. Ma called at this moment of crisis. She has the largest repertoire of fancy Bengali vegetarian dishes. Some of them are so fancy that at one point of time when I still wore pigtails, I was not even sure if those dishes were really Bengali. I mean, when you hear a 'roast', you kind of imagine winter evenings with a warm glowing fire and fat boars turning on spits. But Ma made a phulkopir roast in the pressure cooker of all things. She also made succulent kaanchkolar kofta, chhanar kalia and a killer aloor dom.

After several phone calls I finally settled on aloor dom. Potatoes had a global ring to them and there was nothing that you could do to potatoes that would make people hate them. Humans love potatoes.

The Bangali aloor dom is a star on its own and a supernova when served in certain combinations. My mother made aloor dom with new baby potatoes – soft-skinned and smelling of earth – and served it with hot puffed luchi on Sunday mornings; with a fragrant yellow pulao whose grains glistened with ghee when she was hosting guests; and even as a side with the bhoger khichuri that perfumed the air on Lakshmi Pujo. She made aloor dom in two ways. One is the satvik niramish manner which prohibits the use of onion and garlic in food because of their aphrodisiac properties. This was cooked mostly on one of umpteen religious days. The other method does have its share of alliums but is worth every tear you shed while chopping an onion. I zeroed in on the second one for the party. Cooked with onion, garam masala and spices, aloor dom was going to be my contribution.

Yes, this is how I was going to get a foothold in the international food scene: with a pot of brown masala–coated aloor dom for Thanksgiving. Redolent with the scent of garam masala and ghee, the baby potatoes are best enjoyed with fluffy luchi or soft paranthas. If nothing else, serve with some bread to mop up those tantalizing masalas.

ALOOR DOM
Baby potatoes in a spicy gravy

12 small round potatoes. I used the baby red ones. For larger potatoes you need to increase the spices.

Spices for frying potatoes:
1 tsp ginger garlic paste
1 tsp red chilli powder
½ tsp turmeric powder
¼ tsp salt
1 tsp vegetable oil

For tempering:
2 bay leaves
¼ tsp hing/asafoetida

For the masala:
1 heaped tbsp onion paste
1 medium tomato, pureed
1 tsp cumin powder
½ tsp turmeric powder
½ tsp loosely packed garam masala

½ tsp red chilli powder (you can add more if you like spicy food)
1 heaped tsp ginger paste
2 green chillies chopped in rounds
1 tbsp yoghurt
  Salt to taste. A pinch of rock salt at the end adds zing to the dish
1 tsp sugar (you could use less) loosely packed
2 tbsp oil
1 tsp ghee or less (this is optional, but it does lend a good flavour)

For garnishing:
  Fresh coriander leaves, chopped

- ♪ In a boiling pot or pan, bring water to boil with a little salt. Add the potatoes to it.

- ♪ Once the potatoes are fork-tender, take them out, put them under cold running water and peel them.

- ♪ Prick the potatoes gently and then toss them with the 'spices for frying potato': ginger-garlic paste, red chilli powder, turmeric powder, salt and a little oil. Heat 1 tbsp oil in a frying pan/kadhai. Fry the potatoes till they take on golden-brown spots. Remove and keep aside.

    Hint: I would suggest using a non-stick pan for this dish. Then you can easily sauté the potatoes with less oil.

- ♪ Heat one more tbsp oil in the same pan. Add bay leaves and hing. Add the onion paste and fry with sugar till the onion turns a pinkish brown. This takes around 3–4 min.

- ♪ Add the tomato puree and fry till it is nicely mashed up and well integrated with the onion. Again 4–5 minutes. Add the ginger paste and green chilli.

- ♪ Mix the cumin powder, turmeric powder, garam masala powder and red chilli powder with yoghurt, then lower the heat and add the mixture to the kadhai. Remove kadhai from heat for a couple of minutes because yoghurt tends to curdle in the heat.

- ♪ Sauté the masala till you see the oil separate from it.

- ♪ Add the fried potatoes and toss well so that they are coated with masala. Add very little water (1 cup) and salt and cook till the water almost dries up to give way to a thick and moist gravy. Sprinkle a little rock salt if you wish.

- ♪ Drizzle a tsp ghee on the top and garnish with fresh, chopped coriander leaves.

Alternate satvik niramish option: Temper the oil with bay leaf, dry red chilli, a small piece of star anise, a few whole fenugreek seeds and hing. Follow with the tomatoes, skipping the onion. For the masala, use 1 tbsp bhaja masala along with half a tbsp coriander powder.

> *Sometimes onion paste tends to get bitter. In such cases, chop the onion in chunks, fry till the onion is soft and pink and then cool and make a paste. You can also chop the onion, boil until soft and then cool to make a paste. I usually make such pastes and keep in the refrigerator for quick use during the busy work week.*

NARKEL DIYE PHULKOPIR ROAST
Cauliflower roast with coconut

The resounding success of my aloor dom made me bolder. My next project was a Bengali cauliflower roast. Now, if I leave out the predicate 'narkel diye' or 'with coconut' in the above phrase, this would be my mother's recipe. Or again, maybe it wouldn't.

Ma would often make cauliflower roast during winter. She would do it in the pressure cooker, how or why I do not know. It would smell headily of ghee, whole garam masala, and sharp ginger – welcome smells amidst the naphthalene scented monkey caps I refused to wear. A surfeit of whole garam masala was supposed to warm you up during the cold winter months. With some cloves, cardamom and cinnamon in your blood and a woolen scarf tied under your chin, you were all set to survive the measly winter that Bengal offered.

She made this dish more often when we lived in colder climes, where the temperature would dip close to zero and a coal angithi was not enough to warm the mist that swirled through the window on its descent from the Kanchenjunga. It was there, atop the hills, that she made soups with chunks of vegetable which I hated and this phulkopir roast with bits of whole spices peeking among the white florets.

Later when we moved to the warmer winter of the plains, the dish was not made that frequently.

In all the years that I have tried making this dish, I have never been able to get the pressure cooker to cook the cauliflower right. It would oscillate between mush and extreme crunchiness. Frustrated, I shifted my strategy and started to roast the cauliflower in the oven instead. A quick question on Facebook saw the addition of coconut to Ma's age old dish. I tweaked it sufficiently to make it different from my mother's, and yet, when done, the dish tastes exactly like hers did, in that robust Hawkins pressure cooker that hissed on the hilltop.

If you have the confidence, you can do the whole thing in the pressure cooker too. You can also skip the coconut if you are not fond of it.

1   small cauliflower

Make a marinade as follows:

½   cup thick yoghurt

½   tsp ginger paste

½   tsp garlic paste

½   tsp Kashmiri mirch (or red chilli powder)

½   tsp fresh garam masala powder

Salt to taste

1   tsp olive oil

1   cup chopped onion

1   fat garlic clove or 2 regular

Whole spices for tempering:

- 1 bay leaf
- 1" cinnamon stick
- 2 cloves
- 2 green cardamom
- 4–5 whole black peppercorns (optional)

- 2 tbsp cashew
- 4–5 green chillies

- 1 medium tomato
- ½ cup coconut milk
- Salt to taste
- ½ tsp sugar
- 1 tbsp + 1 tsp vegetable oil
- 1 tsp ghee
- Use grated coconut and raisins for garnish

꙳ Chop cauliflower in large florets. The florets should be about 2" in length and there will be about 10–12 such florets. Dunk them in warm, salted water for 10–15 minutes.

꙳ In a large, wide mouthed bowl, add yoghurt, ginger-garlic paste, kashmiri mirch, garam masala and salt for the marinade. Whip to a smooth paste. Remove the cauliflower florets from the water and put them in the above bowl. Drizzle about 1 tsp olive oil on top. Mix gently till the florets are well coated with the marinade. Let it sit for 30 minutes.

꙳ Heat 1 tsp oil in a frying pan. Fry the onion and garlic till the onion is soft and brown at the edges. Cool and make a paste. Add this to the above marinade and mix well.

Note: You can add raw onion paste, but I like to fry the onion and then make a paste.

꙳ Now arrange the florets in a single layer on a baking tray and bake covered at 350–375 F for about 30 minutes, or till you see the florets browning a little. Bake uncovered for the last ten minutes. If you do not have an oven, lightly sauté the cauliflower florets.

꙳ Heat 1 tbsp oil and 1 tsp ghee together in a saucier/sauté pan/ kadhai. Temper the oil with whole spices for tempering.

♪ Make a paste of tomato, cashews and green chilli with a splash of water. Add this to the oil. Also add any remaining marinade. Fry till you see the oil surfacing. Now add the baked florets and sauté to mix with masala.

♪ Add coconut milk and ½ cup water, adjust for salt and sugar and cook till the florets are done. They should not be crunchy, but should not mush up either.

♪ Before serving, garnish with lightly roasted grated coconut and raisins. Serve this dish with a jeera rice, a Bengali mishti pulao or with soft parathas.

KANCHKOLAR KOFTA CURRY
Green plantain kofta curry

Speaking of shuddh niramish or strict vegetarian food, I must tell you about the elderly ladies in my family, my grandma's contemporaries who are always eager to feed me lunch on my annual visits home. I adore them and they never, ever complain about the tacky gifts I carry from America.

These ladies also serve the best niramish lunch on this side of the universe. Having lived through an era where Bengali widows faced strict food restrictions that included no onion, no garlic, no non-veg and no musuri'r dal, they have learned the best of niramish cooking and their meals, though constrained, are rich in taste and flavour.

I remember that when these ladies came to lunch, my mother would chalk up an elaborate niramish meal with bitter shukto, mildly sweet chhanar dalna and a reddish-looking spicy kanchkolar kofta. The grandmothers relished those soft, succulent koftas and heaped praise on my mother. Why anyone would prefer the vegetarian option to keema koftas, I could not fathom. Now I know better.

Kanchkolar kofta or green plantain koftas are the invention of the genius Bengali who went vegetarian. Dyspepsia, diarrhoea and Digene-obsessed Bengalis rely heavily on kanchkola. Kanchkolar patla jhol, a bland soupy dish, is the Bong anecdote to a night of raucous eating. But for the more enterprising, there is the rich kofta, a clever mimic of meatballs. I learned to cook it from my Ma, who has this wonderful trick of making vegetarian gravy more flavourful with the addition of ginger and hing. This combination gives a beautiful flavour to the oil which infuses the gravy and you will never miss onion or garlic in that melange.

To make the koftas:

- 2 firm green plantains chopped in thirds
- ½ medium sized potato
- ¼ tsp turmeric powder
- 1/3 cup finely chopped onion (optional)
- 2–3 finely chopped green chilli
- 1 tsp minced ginger
- ½ tsp cumin powder
- ¼ tsp dry roasted coriander powder
- ¼ tsp garam masala
- ¼ tsp sugar
  Salt to taste (¼ tsp or more)
- 1 tbsp vegetable oil
- 1 tbsp maida if needed.
- 15 golden raisins

For the gravy:

- 2 tsp ginger paste
- 1/8 tsp hing/asafoetida

Whole garam masala:

- 2 cardamom
- 2 clove
- 2 small bay leaves
- 1" thin stick cinnamon
- ¾ cup tomato puree
- 1 tsp cumin powder
- 1 tsp coriander powder
- ½ tsp or more red chilli powder (Kashmiri mirch if you want the colour and less heat) to taste
- ½–1 tsp turmeric powder
- ¼ tsp garam masala powder
- ½ tsp sugar
  Salt to taste
- 1–2 tbsp cream (optional)
- 2 tbsp vegetable oil + enough for frying the koftas
- 1 tsp ghee

Making the kofta balls

♪ Pressure cook the green plantain and potatoes with about ¼ tsp turmeric powder. This usually takes 3 minutes at full pressure.

♪ Once it is cooked, drain the water completely, remove the peel and mash the plantains together till smooth. Mash the potatoes.

♪ Heat 1 tbsp oil in a frying pan/kadhai.

♪ Add finely chopped onion, green chilli and minced ginger. Fry till onion is soft and pink, browning on the edges. You can skip the onion for a total niramish option.

♪ Next add cumin powder, coriander powder, garam masala, the mashed plantain, mashed potato, sugar and salt to taste. Sauté for 2–3 minutes at medium heat till the masalas mix nicely with the mashed plantain and the mash is dry enough.

♪ Add about 1 tbsp maida to the mash and mix well so that it is tight. Now cool and then make small, gooseberry-sized balls. Stuff each ball with a plump golden raisin. You should be able to make about 12–14 balls.

Frying the balls:

♪ Deep fry the balls in hot oil. Remove with a slotted spoon and keep aside. Assuming that you will eat some of the fried koftas, we will make enough gravy for 10 koftas!

Note: Sometimes if the balls are not tight enough I make a batter with ¼ cup besan, salt and ¼ cup water. Dip the balls in the batter to get a coating and then deep fry.

Making the gravy:

♪ Heat 2 tbsp oil and ½ tsp ghee in a deep bottomed pan/kadhai.

♪ In a small bowl, mix ginger paste and hing. Temper the oil with the above and sauté for half a minute till you can smell the hing.

♪ Add the whole garam masala. Sauté for a minute.

🎵 To the tomato puree add cumin powder, coriander powder, red chilli powder (or Kashmiri mirch), turmeric powder, sugar and salt. Mix. Add this to the oil and fry for about 6–7 minutes at medium heat till you see the oil separate from the masala.

🎵 Now add little more than 1 cup warm water and let the gravy come to a boil. At this point, adjust salt and spices. Once the gravy has come to the desired consistency, lower the heat and add cream. The cream is my addition and not traditional.

🎵 Lower the heat and add the koftas to the gravy. Let the koftas cook in the gravy for a couple of minutes. Switch off and remove from heat. Add fresh garam masala powder and ghee and cover. Serve in the next 10 minutes. If you intend to serve it later, put koftas in the gravy only at the time of serving. The koftas tend to soak up the gravy the longer they are there.

🎵 If you find adding koftas to the gravy tricky, I have found that it is easier to arrange the koftas in the serving dish, pour the gravy on them, let it sit for 30 minutes and then serve.

The New Bengali Vegetarian in a Box

While I was cooking aloor dom and soft koftas from mashed green plantain, trying to create an insulated cocoon of food culture, my daughters were growing up craving mac and cheese and long strands of spaghetti. To be honest, they did love their rice and jhol but I was hyper, insisting they like 'this' better than 'that'. At times there was war. I knew I was slipping into the role of the quintessential immigrant mother and soon 'No sleepovers, only A+ grades and Bhagvad Gita class every Sunday morning' would become my mantra.

Perhaps because I live far from home I desperately try

to stick to the traditions, life and food from my childhood. I care and fret about them even though I hardly remember them. I glamourize the sepia images with swathes of brighter colours and insist that my daughters eat dhokar dalna for dinner. Only, my dhokar dalna never turned out quite right. The lentil-cakes had a mind of their own. They decided to crumble on frying and the brown crunchy specks just disintegrated in the hot oil. The cakes were never firm, though the crumbly mix tasted just right and was eaten by the fistful.

So when Ma visited, bringing with her packets of a readymade dhoka mix — a new product in the Kolkata market — I was suspicious, but relieved. On her visits, I look forward to the suitcases, bulging and heavy, smelling strongly of a life I have left behind. They are stuffed with small brown bottles of homeopathic medicine with handwritten labels, long, rectangular boxes of Boroline, the year's *Ponjika*, the almanac with its smudgy typefaces and sheer jacaranda pink cover, a stack of *Desh* periodicals that has already been well thumbed. Then of course there is the mandatory ghee, kasundi, chanachur and everything edible neatly tucked between the tangails and the valkalams, assuring me that my world is unchanged.

The dhokar dalna — readymade and emerging from a box — was like a gift from the genie and yet not something I could take to with complete trust. In my mind it is a complex affair, a collage of pictures where the dal is being ground in our Sumeet mixer with the blades making a ruckus against the steel jar or more politely on the sil-batta, Ma or Dida making the fried dhoka (which I love to eat plain) and then the dhokar dalna with its faint smell of hing and perfect bay leaf fluttering in gravy. It needs a lot of emotion, touching, tasting and an atmosphere of bonhomie.

Though Ma's dhokar dalna is no doubt exemplary, the 'dhokar dalna' that fleets across my senses is one from a small 'Paise Hotel', so named because of its cheap fixed-rate menu, in Siliguri. This was the late 70s, a period when Bengali food was the prissy, proper maiden, conventional and only available at home. What was available as Bengali restaurants were the numerous 'Bhaater Hotel', small shanty hotels that served rice, dal, charchari, fish curry and such but were not decent enough to visit with family.

So the first time I had a complete Bengali meal outside home was at this 'Paise Hotel' in Siliguri. The hotel was close to the station and very popular for its fish curries. It was a very simple, spartan setup, unlike any restaurant you can conjure in your mind. Long rickety wooden tables and simple rustic chairs made up the seating arrangements. The day's menu was scrawled on a chalkboard and there was nothing fancy on it. The food was akin to home-cooked Bengali food and fish like chitol and pabda was where the main attraction lay. I was at an age where I disliked fish. Instead, it was the neat squares of lentil infused with spices in a reddish coloured silky gravy – their dhokar dalna – that captured my love.

The second time I had dhokar dalna in a restaurant was in Haridwar. I was probably in middle school when we went to Haridwar one winter vacation because my grandmother – Thamma – wished for a religious retreat. After the evening arati by the shimmering, clear waters of the Ganga, dressed in full sleeved sweaters, monkey caps, woolen mufflers and Kashmiri shawls like every other Bengali tourist, we elbowed our way through narrow lanes thick with stores selling brass knick-knacks and pickles to arrive at Dada Boudir Hotel, an unpretentious Bengali restaurant bang in the middle of Uttarakhand. The food was home food at its best. Once we had managed to grab a seat, the server, a small boy, set the table with steel plates, slices of deep green lime, salt and steel tumblers of water. Then came the steaming rice, faint wisps of smoke still swirling through the perfect mound. On that they poured generous dollops of grainy, pure ghee whose colour was like the rich tussar silk and ladlefuls of yellow dal. Piping hot beguni – where the purple skin of the eggplant peeked through the crunchy brown cover – was served as a side. Since this was Haridwar, food was strictly vegetarian and the gravy dish was usually the Bengali chhanar dalna with soft pieces of paneer in a mildly sweet gravy or the more sedate, bourgeois dhokar dalna with a hint of hing and garam masala. The meal always ended with a sweet-sour chaatni and mishti doi. It was the kind of place you could completely trust to give you the best dhokar dalna without any intervention from your mother.

Times have changed since then. In his e-mails, my baba talks about fancy Bengali restaurants that are cooking up a 'Kal-Boishakhi' in the Bengali culinary scene. Bong food is becoming more comfortable in its new sassy avatar and dhokar dalna is being fine-tuned and inserted into a box. Ma, however, believes her recipe is still the best.

I agree.

After Ma had left I was hit with this urge to cook dhokar dalna again. The 'dalna' or gravy part of the dish was a breeze, a mellow spring zephyr which I could manage with eyes shut. The crux of the problem lay in the 'dhoka'. No wonder it has been named thus – it is a total fraud case. The harder I tried to make it, the more it crumbled. The crumbles were delicious and I had no qualms in eating them up but all I was doing was eating loads of perfectly delicious lentil crumbles while the dhoka remained unmade.

'Show me exactly what you mean by "little water for paste". I am going nowhere with this thing,' I wailed to Ma, who was now leading her busy social life in Kolkata.

So we met on Skype, one weeknight after the kids had been bathed and fed. I had the chholar dal and motor dal ready, having soaked them overnight. I had signed on to Skype on my iPad and was waiting for Ma to pop up on screen.

'Okay, now drain the water and put it in the blender,' I could suddenly hear her voice but the screen was blank.

'Adjust your webcam, I can't see anything!' I shouted. The screen now showed a slice of pale blue wall with a framed photo of Tagore.

'You have focused it on the wall. Turn the webcam, turn, turn!'

My mother's face replaced the blue wall, out of focus, she was looking away and flapping her hands furiously. This time I couldn't hear anything.

'No, no, you haven't mopped under that table, that one…' the audio came back with a sputter.

'Ma, Ma… concentrate!'

'Arre, Manu'r Ma will have to leave, no? Now you put the dal in the blender along with the green chilli and add water, very little at a time. Start with only half cup water.'

Ma was still looking away, her heart clearly under the table rather than in the dhoka.

While my mother made sure the corners got dusted, I made the lentil paste. This time I was careful with the water and a thick smooth paste ensued. I was happy.

'Look, Ma... the paste looks good, na?' I thrust the bowl at the screen.

'Why are you wearing such small shorts? Chhi, chhi, your daughters are getting older, what will they think? What will I do with you? You have to dry the dhoka but add the moshla first,' Ma said, exasperated and still out of focus. I could see her head shaking.

I added cumin powder, ginger paste, salt and a little bit of sugar to the lentil paste and whipped it up like soufflé batter.

I put a kadhai on the stove and added a teaspoon of oil.

'Arre, add more oil. What are you making, granola bars or what?' Ma giggled at her own joke.

I added another teaspoon. Hing and cumin seeds danced around in the hot oil. Ma disappeared again, probably to inspect the undersides of the bed, couch and fridge for specks of dirt.

I added the lentil paste and started stirring it. Ma was still MIA.

Almost five minutes later, she came into view, or at least her glasses did.

'Lower the heat, low, low. Now keep stirring till it comes off nicely from the sides. Almost like a dough it will start looking.'

In the next ten minutes, the paste started coming together.

'Taste the dough. Make sure it is not raw. Pour it out on a greased plate and then with your hand fashion a round cake-like mound. Cut out diamonds just like those kaju barfi you love. Remember how many of those you would eat. You put on so much weight just eating those barfis.'

I had made almost-perfect diamonds of spiced lentils. This was easy, yes, it was actually quite simple.

'Now you can bake or fry them. When you fry, heat enough oil and shallow fry both sides till golden. See, it was easy. You never pay attention when I am making these things. Just like your dad you have become. It's because you don't take those fish oil capsules I keep telling you to.' Ma was finally sharp and focused, and was peering into my dhoka.

'You need to do this more often. Practice makes the dhoka perfect,' was her parting shot.

DHOKAR DALNA
Spiced lentil cakes in a gravy

For the dhoka:
1¼ cup chholar dal (chana dal)
¼ cup matar dal (yellow split peas)
1 tsp roasted cumin powder
1½ tsp ginger paste
4 green chillies
¾ tsp cumin seeds
¼ tsp hing/asafoetida
Salt to taste
¼ tsp sugar
6–8 tbsp oil

For the gravy:
1 potato chopped in eights
2 small bay leaves
½ tsp whole cumin seeds
¼ tsp hing
1 tomato finely chopped or pureed
1 tsp fresh ginger paste or grated ginger
1 tsp yoghurt
1 tsp cumin powder
1 tsp coriander powder

1 tsp red chilli powder, or according to taste	Salt to taste
½–1 tsp turmeric powder	¼ tsp garam masala powder
½ tsp sugar	1 tbsp oil
	1 tsp ghee

♪ Soak chana dal and matar dal in four cups of water overnight. The next day, drain the water and put the dal in the blender along with the green chilli. Slowly adding water, make a smooth paste. The paste should not be too liquidy, so start with ½ cup water and then add more as needed.

♪ Add roasted cumin powder, ginger paste, salt and ¼ tsp sugar to the dal paste. Mix well with a fork.

♪ Now heat 2 tbsp oil in a kadhai or frying pan. I prefer to do this in a non-stick frying pan as I can cook the mix easily without much sticking. Temper the oil with cumin seeds and hing. In 2 minutes the spices will start sputtering.

♪ Add the dal paste to the frying pan and lower the heat. At low-medium heat, keep stirring continuously till the dal paste starts coming off the sides easily. Add a little oil if necessary. In around 9–10 minutes you will see the paste has come together and is coming off the sides easily. This step is really tricky. You need to stir vigorously, else the paste will stick to the sides and you need to be careful to remove the moisture without making it hard. In a couple of minutes it should be done. You can take little morsels and taste to see that the paste is now cooked and no longer raw.

♪ Now grease a plate and pour the almost dried but soft dal paste on it. With the palm of your hand, flatten the top and make a round or rectangular cake-like shape about ¾–1" in height. If the dough still feels like it has too much moisture, pop it in the oven for two-three minutes at 350 F. Cut diamond-shaped pieces from this. You will get around 20 pieces of lentil cakes of which you will probably eat some after frying.

♪ To fry these pieces heat 5 tbsp oil and shallow fry the dhoka pieces till golden brown on both sides.

Making the gravy

♪ Heat the oil and the ghee. Fry the potatoes with a pinch of turmeric and remove to be added later.

♪ Temper with bay leaf, cumin seeds and hing. In a minute, the spices will sputter.

♪ Reduce heat to medium and add tomato puree and ginger paste. Fry this tomato-ginger combination for 6–8 minutes. Sprinkle a little water if necessary. At the end you will see the oil seeping out from the edges.

♪ In a bowl, mix yoghurt, cumin powder, coriander powder, turmeric powder and red chilli powder to a smooth paste. Remove the kadhai from heat and then add masala paste to avoid curdling yoghurt. Sauté for a minute. Now put the kadhai back on medium heat and fry masala for the next two minutes.

♪ Add the potatoes, mix and add 1–2 cups of warm water. Add salt to taste. Add sugar. Let the gravy simmer and come to a boil. Cover and cook till potatoes are done. Taste and adjust for seasoning. Now let the gravy simmer for a couple more minutes.

♪ Gently immerse the fried dhoka pieces in the gravy. Let it simmer for a couple of minutes. Now sprinkle garam masala powder and ghee. Switch off the heat and keep covered. Serve warm within the next 30 minutes.

♪ If you plan to serve later, it is best to add the dhoka pieces to the gravy and let them simmer in there right before serving.

Note: Tomatoes were not a widely used vegetable in Bengali cuisine until the late twentieth century. They were also seasonal vegetables available only in winter. The thick gravy dishes like dalna were made without tomatoes and only based on spices. I use tomatoes as I feel they accentuate the taste.

When making dalna or any other gravy-based dish, it is a good idea to mix the dry spice powders like cumin and coriander in a little water or yoghurt and then add the spice paste to the dish.

The Mustard Tales

Mustard as a spice is an important part of Indian cooking. For Bengalis it is as important as air; they cannot live without it. When they travel to unknown locales they carry bottles of this oil tucked in their suitcases, carefully wrapped in cream coloured Kashmiri shawls.

In many parts of India, the whole mustard seeds are used for tempering, to add flavour to the oil. Bengalis go several steps further and use the oil, paste, leaves and seeds in their cooking. In most Bengali or East Indian cooking, mustard oil is used as the cooking medium. Shorshe bata or mustard paste is an ubiquitous ingredient in Bengali cuisine. The mustard seeds are ground to a wet paste with green chilli and salt to make a pungent, sharp paste which is used to make the sauce in many Bengali dishes. When done in a grinder, the paste tends to get bitter. To avoid this, try the following: use yellow mustard which has less sharpness, and while making paste, add green chilli, salt and a little posto.

If I stir my soul with a ladle and ask myself, 'Would you have cooked these Bengali meals if you were not a mother?' I know what I will say. Without batting an eyelid I will say 'No. I would rather rest my feet and watch Alton Brown cook an omelette and order in Thai food instead'. As food-crazy as I may be, I like it best when it is cooked by someone else.

At the most I would have made an aloor dom here and a doi maachh there, I would have thrown parties once a year and entertained with kosha mangsho, but never would I have striven so hard to build a kitchen that smells so strongly of pungent mustard and sweet paanch-phoron that you need a vent fan in high speed to breathe easy.

I tell myself I want to set up new traditions and yet I tend to go back and follow the routines that my mother and her mother followed. In a different setting, my methods are milder but I still make paayesh on birthdays, chicken curry in a pressure cooker on Sundays, ghee at home albeit from organic butter.

Mint, coriander, cardamom, cumin: these are the smells, the tastes I want my daughters to remember their home by. Yes, I could make pasta and pour Ragu sauce on it and make a tradition out of that too. But those scents are unfamiliar to me. And as much as I like pasta, I cannot bear the thought of a jar of Ragu sauce reminding my daughters of me.

For the exact same reasons, I don't even venture to be the next Nigella Lawson. Okay, who am I kidding?

Instead I strive to be the Bong Mom, the mother with a bolder, spicier, warmer flavour. This is the reason I plod along resiliently and when my younger one, with curls framing her tiny face, wants to see what is the 'sizzling' sound in the kitchen, I hoist her on the countertop and hand her a stick of brown cinnamon. She holds it close to her nose and takes in the smell, her head nodding appreciatively. My oldest was wont to sit on the countertop, pounding cardamom and cloves in my stone mortar till she turned all of five. 'Why is it not hot, you said garam masala, garam means hot.' She would say the entire time.

I bear all of it with clenched teeth and on-the-go kapaalbhaati. I take deep breaths and try to do power yoga when little Miss French cuisine asks 'Eta ki?' pointing with distrust at her food. 'Lobster thermidor,' I say, while I make morsels of dal-bhaat and aloo-beans tarkari.

And then I introduce them to fish, an important part of my being.

If I recall correctly it was not me who introduced my daughters to fish. It was my mother, or maybe my mother-in-law, who had the gall to insist that I feed my babies a lunch of fish curry and rice at six months. Yes, fish curry to my precious baby otherwise destined to eat organic peas pulped into a gooey green mess. The pediatrician did not concur. She wanted to stick to a familiar Western diet and not wade into fishy waters until the child turned at least a year old.

I wanted to stick to the pediatrician. After all, she was the one getting all my insurance money.

But Indian women are tough, especially grandmothers. So, while I tried hard to come up with a healthy stew brimming with vegetables, homemade apple sauce and free range organic chicken soup, the grandmothers fed the child bits and pieces of fish like rui or pabda or tyangda from their own lunch plates. Soon, the crawling child could be seen sitting by the dining table, waiting patiently for her share of fish during grandma's lunch and she didn't even have to wag a tail.

The child was losing all interest in my organic chicken soup and mashed carrots. TRP was falling fast. The kid wanted to know the recipe behind every bit of goop I served up. 'Eta ki diyechho?' was her standard question at every meal. In the face of a chicken korma and doi maachh I stood little chance.

And then what I dreaded happened. We were at a dinner. The hostess was a tree hugging-free range-bonded to vegetables-organic-local mom. Her children asked for carrot sticks at snack and ate a plateful of grilled asparagus with unadulterated enthusiasm. She knew every parenting book by rote and commented voraciously on everything posted at BabyCenter. These are the kinds you steer clear of if you are not moi.

That evening, before setting out dinner for the adults, she suggested that the kids have their meal. Brilliant idea. Not. Bright colourful plastic plates and tumblers were set out. Cheerful napkins with letters of the alphabet printed on them were neatly stacked. Steamed spears of broccoli with a sprinkle of grated parmesan were served as starters. While everyone else munched on them happily, my then two year old pointed at it with suspicion and enquired, 'Eta ki?'

'Broccoli,' I muttered under my breath. The other mom was throwing me suspicious looks. I mean, which two year old does not know a broccoli piece when she sees it? Two year olds are supposed to know nothing but broccoli! It was all my fault.

'Ami gachh khai na, giraffes khay!' The spawn of my womb declared with great resolution that she did not eat plants, but giraffes did.

The mushroom soup did not have much luck either. A few spoonfuls of macaroni and cheese later the child was still hungry.

'She doesn't eat very healthy, does she? You should have introduced her to better food early,' the hostess said. I gave my best grim smile. Who will judge what is better?

When the food for the grownups was served, my prodigy was on a roll. She ate the fish fry, the spicy fish kaalia, slurped the raita and fell in love with the tandoori chicken. From the far end of the dining room, the grandmother flashed a proud smile.

Fishy Fishy Bong Bong

*'Give a man a fish and you feed him for a day. Teach
a man to fish and you feed him for a lifetime.'*
— Chinese proverb

*This will not work for the average Bong. The Bong
Man will never fish, but he might tell you 'Pleesh
come to my house, I make very good pheesh, you
sheet and I make pheesh for you.'
Don't worry. I will tell you how to make better fish
than that.*

It was one of those uninspiring days at work. People talked incessantly at meetings and discussed strategies. The office blonde had on the scariest shade of cherry-pink lipstick I have ever seen and was trying to sell Girl Scout cookies in the midst of all this. While words like 'synergic productivity', 'high performance' and 'peanut pink cookies' were flung around like confetti, I doodled fish motifs on my iPad. An arc morphed into fish scales, patterned fins and then a whole smiling fish. People do far worse things at work, like picking noses or playing Angry Birds, but we won't discuss such fishy business here. We will stick to plain ole fish.

Fish has been my longtime weakness and surprisingly one of the things I learned to cook pretty early. I could make a basic maachher jhol around the same time that I learned to make dal. I still could not gut a fish or clean its innards, but I could deftly remove scales, fry it with turmeric and salt and then make a jhol out of it. So cooking doi maachh or bhapa ilish came quite naturally to me and I enjoyed it as much as the H-man hated the fish smell (he went around the house spraying room freshener and opening windows on my 'fish-cooking' days).

'What is this stench? What did you make? Did you not throw away that mouldy Brie from last year?' the H-man enquires, sniffing the air as soon as he enters the house. 'Is it fish? Again?' I switch the vent to high, drowning out his concerns while I make my maachher kaalia.

My older daughter took to fish with an eagerness that amazed me. Being born across the Hudson and not on the banks of the Ganga, her taste in fish naturally differs from mine. She loves the pale pink of salmon or the firm white fillets of tilapia. She loves them baked in a slurry of olive oil and lemon juice, with a sprinkle of herbed salt. When it comes to fish like rui or ilish (hilsa) her foreign fear of bones takes over. She hasn't learned to tease the flesh in her mouth and search for the bones with the tip of her tongue, so she prefers to remain in the safety of boneless fish fillets. She is slowly learning to appreciate the ambrosial taste of the ilish, but the primal fear is still there.

That day, though, I had a strong urge to rise above the salmon in my refrigerator. I wanted to feel the softness of ilish coated in mustard sauce in my mouth. I wanted to crush the green chillies into the rice with a press of my thumb and mix the daffodil-yellow gravy with my fingers. So it was no surprise when my car took a detour that afternoon and followed the exit towards the Indian subcontinent taped bang in the middle of New Jersey.

No sooner had my car turned right at the signal where the exclusive Indian neighbourhood begins, than there was a radical change in the surroundings. Slightly shabby looking stores with smudged glass fronts and names like Dimple and Dakshin dotted the street. Auntyjis dressed in sequinned salwar-kameez that dazzled in the sunlight crossed my path without waiting for the Walk sign to flash. The road was littered with crumpled paper and plastic bags and cars were double-parked at all the wrong places. Above this rose the faint smell of biryani loaded with spices and the syrupy scent of orange jalebis bobbing in hot oil. I took a deep breath and the heart heaved a sigh as the sense of familiarity seeped in.

When I pushed the glass doors of Ahmed's Halal Fish & Meat, sandwiched between a saree shop and a sweet store, a light tinkle of bells announced my arrival. It was dark inside and I pushed my sunglasses up. A heavy scent of incense hung around the room, trying its best to shroud the fishy odour. Ahmed bhai was at his place behind the formica-topped counter, gazing intently at the small LCD TV screen. 'Salaam Alekum apa', he said, his accent still ringing of Narayanganj from where he had emigrated twenty years ago, and continued staring at the screen. It looked like a Bangladeshi soap was on. A young girl, her hair plaited and in double folds, was reciting animated dialogues amidst soul-jarring music. It seemed utterly wrong to disturb Ahmed bhai at this moment and ask for the going price of hilsa.

So I waited quietly, turning my concentration to the screen. I am not totally ignorant of Bangladeshi soaps. There was a time when we had only two channels back home, DD1 and DD2. DD2 was the Bengali channel, its programmes were transmitted from Kolkata. Other than the Bengali Cinema on Saturdays and a children's programme called 'Harek Rakamba', it had little else to offer. Most evenings they devoted time to boring discussions or a half-hour agricultural programme called *Krishi Sangbad*. As a result of this, many of our Bengali neighbours had a double antenna, the second of which caught Bangla channels from Bangladesh. Bangladeshi serials, natok as we called them, were thought to be of high reputation. That they also transmitted Western serials like *Dallas* and *Different Strokes* was an added bonus.

Our antenna, however, had a slight problem. There was a big banyan tree in front of our home, with widespread branches which apparently messed with the signals from Bangladesh that the antenna was designed to catch. Every few days Baba had to climb on the roof and rotate the antenna a wee bit to make it serve its purpose. It wasn't totally strange to hear us shouting out instructions, our upper bodies stretched across the window, 'More, more – ar ektu, ar ektu!' Then an elated 'Hoyeche, hoyeche' when done and finally a dejected 'Jah, chole gelo' on the repeated loss of the signal while Baba in his pyjamas rotated the antenna.

In spite of this, Ma followed Bangla natoks from Bangladesh on snowy TV screens and claimed they got better after 9:30 at night. She had her own theory about how signals got stronger at night when everyone in Bangladesh went to bed.

Back to the store: Ahmed bhai finally realized that I was waiting and asked me what I wanted. I made obvious my shock at the high price of hilsa which used to be really cheap just a few years ago, and finally placed an order for a three-pounder.

I planned to make bhapa ilish for dinner, nestled in yellow mustard sauce, doused with mustard oil and hot green chillies; it is a quick affair if you do it in the oven. Even as the screeching sound of the electric saw cut through the frozen fish, my mind rolled back a decade...

When I came to the US twelve years ago, I did not crave fish. I thought a double cheeseburger at McDonald's was gourmet food and was happy to have it every day. 'Please, I don't eat beef,' I said repeatedly on the mike at the drive-through. By the time I realized I should have hollered 'No beef!' to make myself understood, I had already eaten half-a-dozen beefy cheeseburgers. Ten days later I started missing maachher jhol and by the twelfth day I was seriously craving some fish. The seafood section at the grocery store did not help much. There were crabs with hard shells trained to predict World Cup wins, huge lobsters and pale pink fillet of fish I had never even heard of. With a stem of parsley here and a lemon rind there it all looked pretty; but the salmon that we got hit my nerves with its bold flavours and salty sea smell.

I was used to sweet river fish and this was not my idea of what fish should taste like.

It was in this frustrated, fishless state of mind that I met N, my first Bong friend in the US. I cringe now when I think of the way I befriended her.

It had been more than two months since we had arrived and I was yet to meet a single Bengali soul. How I pined to gossip in Bengali, to chat with someone about Kolkata, to ask someone the best place to buy hilsa. But there was no one.

One such afternoon I was walking the aisles of K-Mart, with nothing better to do, when I heard fragments of Bengali being spoken in the neighbouring aisle. I peered around and saw a young couple, the girl in a salwar-kameez talking animatedly to her husband.

I felt an immense urge to butt in and join their discussion, but I restrained myself. I was frustrated, yes, but still far short of being labelled a lunatic.

I saw them again in the parking lot, lugging something into their trunk and I felt the urge to go up to them again.

My heart lurched and butterflies flapped in my stomach. This time I asked the H–man.

Me: 'Do you think I should go and introduce myself to that couple over there? They are Bangali.'

The H–man: 'What couple?'

Me: 'There. See? The grey Honda. The tall guy loading the trunk.'

The H–man: 'What is that... a Bose?'

Me, frustrated: 'How would I know if they are Bose or Sen, I haven't introduced myself yet. Shall I? They can suggest places to get rui, you know.'

The H–man, eyes glazed: 'Is it the 5.1 channel system or 2.1? Let me run back to the store and check out the price.'

In the meantime, the couple were closing the trunk and getting into the car. In sheer desperation I bolted towards their car, said 'hi', muttered something about me being Bengali and it would be nice if we could meet, etc. and scribbled my number on a scrap of paper and ran. Yeah, I just ran back while they stood there patiently, quizzically...

Then one day she called and as they say, the rest is history. She was the one who introduced me to the Bangladeshi places that sell rui and ilish and tyangra maachh all neatly frozen and the Gujarati lady who does eyebrows for three dollars.

Since then I have found many Bangladeshi fish sellers who stock everything from the Padma river's hilsa to mourala maachh. I have also become used to the fish of the salty sea. These days, I love salmon almost as much as bhetki.

When Ahmed bhai finally handed me the fish pieces, the evening was getting busier. The fish in my bag looked as inanimate as a glass sculpture. That did not fool me. Though it is a far cry from the fresh fish in the rivers of my childhood town, I know that once thawed and fried in some mustard oil, it tastes as good. Not as good as the memories I carry, but it will have to do for now.

Shorshe Ilish Bhaape
Hilsa steamed in mustard sauce

With the first ilish of the season (the permanent winter in Ahmed bhai's freezer in this case) I always itch to make a steamed mustardy shorshe ilish bhaape or a yoghurt-mustard dish of doi shorshe ilish. Those tiny mustard seeds, ground together with green chilli and a pinch of salt, have a power so potent that it is hard to ignore. Surprisingly I never paid much attention to them until I had crossed seven seas and thirteen rivers.

Shorshe bata, ground mustard paste, is one of those small things that you tend to ignore when you live with your parents. I mean, really, who thinks about mustard paste when there is someone to grind it into a fine, watery, mild yellow on your mother's slab of stone that you had very little regard for. When you are twenty, you pity your mother for relying on an ugly slab of stone for grinding her masalas. When you are on the wrong side of thirty, you want to give up your shiny Cuisinart for that piece of rock.

In my case, the situation was worse. I could never get the right taste of shorshe bata in my blender. Heck, the mustard seeds turned stubborn, refusing to give in, to mate with the green chilli and develop a loving companionship. All this until I got that perfect blender with a small jar which made a shorshe bata as good as the one I remembered from my childhood.

And then there was no end to it. I made mustard paste like a woman on a high; soak, whirr, ta-da! A beautiful paste with that sharp smell that goes right up your nose. I was happy, my ilish happier. Nestled in that beautiful sauce, my hilsa gave me their best, a taste so exquisite, so ethereal that it is hard to describe.

To make mustard paste:

2   tbsp mustard seeds
2   tsp poppy seeds
3–4 green chilli
    Salt for the paste
    Soak the above in less than
    ½ cup water for 30 minutes
    and then strain and make a
    smooth paste

4–5 pieces hilsa cut in steak-
    size pieces, washed and
    cleaned of scales etc.
2   tbsp yoghurt
½   tsp turmeric powder
4–5 hot Indian green chilli slit
    Salt to taste
4–5 tsp mustard oil

♪ In a bowl, add the mustard paste, yoghurt, 2 tsp mustard oil, turmeric powder and salt to taste. Mix well. This is the mustard sauce you will use for the fish.

Hint: If you have a bottle of kasundi, add 1–2 tsp kasundi to the mustard paste that you have made. This lends an awesome taste.

Method 1 – In the oven

♪ Grease an oven-safe bowl with a little mustard oil. Place the fish pieces in the bowl in a single layer. Pour the prepared mustard sauce over it so that it covers all the fish pieces nicely. Add 4–5 slit green chillies on the top and drizzle remaining mustard oil on them.

♪ Cover the bowl with an aluminium foil and bake at 375. After 15 minutes remove the cover and bake open until done.

Note: Oven temperatures may vary depending on the make of the oven.

♪ Serve hot with rice.

Method 2 – In the pressure cooker

♪ Smear a pressure cooker-safe bowl with a little mustard oil. Place the fish pieces in the bowl in one single layer. Pour the prepared mustard paste or sauce over it so that it covers all the fish pieces nicely. Add 4 slit green chillies on the top and pour remaining mustard oil on them. Cook in pressure cooker for 2–3 whistles.

Variations: If available, wrap the individual fish pieces in square pieces of fresh banana leaf and then steam in a pressure cooker.

Frying Fish the Bengali Way

Before going deep into fish, I thought I would spend some time describing what exactly Bengalis do to their fish before they add it to various gravies. After cleaning the fish, they rub the fish pieces with turmeric and salt and then let it rest for 20–30 minutes. I usually use ½-1 tsp turmeric powder and ½ tsp salt to marinate 4–5 pieces of fish. Next, the fish has to be fried in oil. Ideally, it should be deep fried in hot mustard oil for the optimum taste. But I prefer to shallow fry the fish in a non-stick pan. I use about 2–3 tbsp oil for frying 4 pieces of fish. To fry fish, the oil needs to be sufficiently hot, otherwise the fish tends to stick. Once the oil is hot, slide fish pieces gently into the oil. The pieces should remain side by side. Flip with a flat spatula once the side is done. Fry till both sides are golden. Also, fish tends to sputter, so go about it carefully.

Maachha Besara
An Odia fish curry

It was one of those days, when I had finished responding to the boss's nth e-mail even though I had called in sick, played the Dora puzzle, wiped my offspring's bottom for the nineteenth time and cooked a chicken stew. My nose was stuffy and red and I had sung 'Rudolph the red-nosed...' to entertain the three-year-old. Just when I was beginning to think that quality time with one's children is highly overrated, I found myself at the computer on a site called Odia Kitchen. There I noticed a fish recipe so different that it completely drew me in and I simply had to make it even thought it was my sick day.

What really attracted me to this dish was the use of garlic with mustard. Never in my Bong life had I come across a dish that used mustard and garlic together. I adapted the recipe to my taste and this different take on mustard has become a family favourite ever since.

4	steak sized pieces of rohu or other freshwater fish	4	tbsp mustard paste. Make mustard paste with 2 tbsp mustard powder mixed with water or grind fresh mustard seeds.
1	potato, peeled and chopped in pieces lengthwise	¾	tsp loosely packed paanch-phoron
¼	cup yoghurt		Salt to taste
6	slit green chillies	1	tsp turmeric powder
1	fat garlic clove or 2 regular fresh coriander leaves for garnish	1	tbsp mustard oil (or any other cooking oil) for gravy and enough oil for frying fish

- Wash the fish well, pat dry and rub with about ½ tsp turmeric powder and a little salt and keep aside.

- Make a paste of yoghurt, 3 green chillies and garlic. Add the mustard paste to it and make a smooth paste.

- Heat enough oil for frying fish in a kadhai. Once the fish is fried to a golden-yellow on both sides, take it out and drain on a paper towel.

- Next, heat 1 tbsp oil in the heated pan and add paanch-phoron and the rest of the green chillies.

- When it starts crackling add the sliced potato and fry for 2–3 minutes.

- Reduce heat to low and add the yoghurt and mustard paste. If you are in fear of the yoghurt curdling, remove the pan from fire and only then add the paste. Wait for 30 seconds and bring the pan back to low heat. Add turmeric and salt. Cook the paste for 2 minutes. Now add about ½ cup warm water. Simmer the gravy for a few minutes till it comes to a boil.

- Once the potatoes are done add fried fish to the curry and simmer for 2 more minutes.

- Garnish with fresh coriander leaves. Serve hot with plain rice.

The Fish

Though I take umbrage if random people ask me what I eat other than fish, the fact that a Bengali eats a lot of fish is not really untrue. Growing up, we were always a family who ate fish for both lunch and dinner most days. A good fish made my mother happy. If she was singing Rabindrasangeet in the kitchen, it could only mean one thing: the fish talked to her.

My rite of passage as a fishy Bong started at the tender age of six months when I was handed a huge fried head of fish on a silver platter. That was my Annaprashan, my moment of introduction to the world of food in a Bengali home. Things got more intense when, as small kids, we were pushed into the barbaric activity of eating fish head with the incentive that devouring it (especially the brain) would enrich our brains and also make our vision stronger. 'Khub buddhi hobe,' my Ma insisted. What I would do with so much intelligence was a question I never asked.

But my personal love affair with fish started only when we moved to a small township on the banks of the river Ganga some time between my tween and teen years.

It was a quiet town, far from the trappings of the city. Life there was slow and the mornings rolled out leisurely like a well rounded luchi. Grocery was not just relegated to weekends; fresh veggies and fish were brought home every morning from the local market which shimmered with vibrant greens, reds and purples on winter mornings.

My father was no gourmand, but the haat beckoned to him and on cold winter mornings he would walk all the way; across the still-wet grass of the football field where the jatra companies, the travelling theatres, had set up their tents, around the small town library to the haat where the farmers from nearby villages would set up their produce. Pristine nun-like white cauliflowers nestled in their green stalks, plump tomatoes snuggled with sexy orange carrots, the wet earth still clinging to their stumps. And then there was the fish, scales glinting in the morning sun like shiny quarters, their tails still flipping the last beats. Most days Baba would come back with big cloth bags filled with a variety of vegetables and a smaller nylon bag with cut pieces of fish like rui or katla. Baba was not adventurous about his fish and always stuck to the larger fish – kaata maachh, as they were called. While the vegetable bag went into the kitchen, the smaller fish bag found its place under the lone water tap in the backyard, where it would be washed every day and dried in the sun to be reused the next morning.

A little later in the day, when the sun was high and the day had fallen into its slow pace only broken by the calls of the ghughoo in the mango tree, the odd fisherman with gleaming silver in his basket would do the rounds of our town to sell his remaining catch. If not satisfied with the morning haul – which was often – my mother would call him over and haggle over the smaller tyangra, mourala or whatever he had. After much amiable chit-chat, both would be happy and Manu'r Ma would be called to sit down with the curved, iron-bladed 'boti' and fish in the backyard. If the fisherman failed to show up, my mother would wait till I came home from school, dust herself with Mysore sandal talc, freshly pleat her saree and then walk to the market where the evening bargaining would be picking up. The house help's son and I tagged along. Amidst eager calls of 'Boudi' from the sellers, Ma would deftly progress to her trusted fishseller. Under the light of the oil lamps, the small fish flickered like silver trinkets. Ma wasn't a good haggler but maintained a façade of bargaining, and we always returned home jubilant with kilos of pabda or parshe.

So most days, there would be different kinds of fish being cooked for lunch and dinner.

During the monsoon, when the river crisscrossing our town ran high, Manu'r Ma's little boy (who spent most

evenings at our home under Ma's tutelage), would spend
his afternoons at the river catching fish with his gamcha
(a thin cotton towel). No doubt it gave him more pleasure
than breaking his head over his fractions or algebra. His
extra catch, mostly shrimp or kucho chingri or small fish
like khoira and punti, would find a home in Ma's kitchen.
They would be fried crisp and eaten with dal or as a spicy
dry dish.

The rains also meant ilish, the famous hilsa that lives
in the sea and swims along rivers to lay its eggs. As the
monsoon progressed and ilshe-guri rain fell in a lacy mist
throughout the day, clothes were hung to dry inside, a damp
rain smell permeated the cement floors and most evenings
Baba came home with a pair of Padma's ilish – a prize catch
from the famous river. Manu'r Ma would be in the kitchen,
cutting and cleaning. Ilish pieces would be fried in smoking,
golden mustard oil later. While the trees arched in the wind
and rain water gurgled through the gutter outside, pooling
into puddles beneath the banyan tree in our garden, our
home turned cozy and fragrant with the smell of roasting
moong dal and fried fish. On those nights, khichuri and
maachh bhaja were on the menu.

Eating so many different kinds of fresh fish in all sorts
of jhol, jhaal, chorchori and whatnot every day, I fell in love
with fish. I also fell in love with the small town which we
had to leave eventually, but my love for such places remains
and I never feel quite at home in a big city.

This story about fish sounds like fiction to my girls. For
them, food and its source are as far removed as Park Street
and Madhyamgram. The only time they have seen live fish
is in large aquariums. Then they are more interested in

knowing if the brightly coloured clown fish is 'Nemo' than in agonizing over where this species figures in our food chain. This trend is not restricted to fish alone. They have seen cows only in petting zoos and goats on TV.

No wonder then that when my youngest was asked, 'Where do you get milk from?' she, with her two years' worth of knowledge, promptly said, 'Refrigerator. Baba puts it there.'

MURI GHONTO
A heady fish head dish

Bengalis eat every inch of the fish, including the head. The head is actually a coveted body part. It was set aside exclusively for the male members of the family in the old days. I don't know if it was a shrewd female ploy to keep the meaty portions for themselves and serve the male the bony head, but that is how the fish head was pushed to stardom.

In this dish, the succulent and juicy head of a sweet river fish like rui or katla is cooked with potatoes and a smattering of rice. It is a delicacy par excellence. In my house we eat it with rice; at my in-laws' the dish is served as a snack and eaten by itself.

Half the head of a regular-sized fresh water fish	2 tsp grated ginger
2 medium potatoes, peeled, chopped and cubed	3 slit green chillies
1/3 cup basmati rice	**For tempering**
1 medium onion ground to a paste	2 small bay leaves
	2 cardamom
	1" cinnamon stick

The spices
- 1 tsp cumin powder
- 1 tsp garam masala powder
- ½ tsp red chilli powder (adjust to taste)
- 1 tsp turmeric powder

Salt to taste
- 1 tsp sugar
- 1 & 1/2 tbsp oil (mustard or other) for the dish. 3 tbsp for frying the fish head
- ½ tsp ghee

♪ Wash and clean fish head, sprinkle salt and ¼ tsp turmeric and let it sit for 15–30 minutes. I use half a regular-sized fish head for fish like rohu or katla.

♪ Heat oil in a kadhai.

♪ Fry the fish head till it turns a nice shade of yellowish brown. While frying, try breaking it into medium sized pieces, so that it is easier to suck on but is not large enough to choke you. Remove and keep aside.

♪ Fry potatoes with turmeric to a light golden, remove and keep aside for about 3 minutes.

♪ Temper the oil with the bay leaf, elaichi and cinnamon stick.

♪ Add the paste of onion and fry with sugar till the oil separates and the onion has taken on a light brownish hue. This should take about four minutes at medium heat. Add fresh grated ginger, green chillies and cumin powder and fry the masala with a sprinkle of water for a couple of minutes. Now add the potatoes. Sprinkle turmeric powder. Sauté for a minute.

♪ Add uncooked and washed basmati rice. If you have gobindobhog (a variety of rice popular in Bengal), it works better.

♪ Fry for a couple of minutes and add the fried fish head pieces.

♪ Add fresh garam masala powder, red chilli powder and salt and mix well. Fry for 5 minutes, sprinkling a little water as needed.

Tip: You can add a little grated nutmeg and lime zest at this point if the fish smell bothers you.

ɓ Add about 1 cup water and cover and cook at low heat. Check to see if you need water in between and stir in between.

ɓ Cook until the rice and potatoes are done. It should be moist but will not have gravy. Top it with a little ghee – it lends a wonderful flavour.

My Ma's Easy Tomato Fish
A quick and easy fish curry cooked in a tomato-based gravy

In winter, when tomatoes were a-plenty and in their freshest, juiciest avatar, Ma would make this curry. With its lovely colour and tangy taste, this was a dish to look out for. She used a teaspoon or two of cream on days that she was entertaining. For us, the everyday people, the cream was one of those things you put down under 'optional'.

2–4	pieces of sweet water fish like rui or katla cut in steak size pieces or filet of salmon.
1	cup fresh tomato puree
3	green chillies
1	tsp ginger paste
1	tsp loosely packed cumin powder
½	tsp turmeric powder

For tempering:

¼	tsp methi/fenugreek seeds
¼	tsp hing/asafoetida
2	small bay leaves

Salt to taste

¼	tsp sugar (or more if needed)
1	tbsp oil for cooking + 2 tbsp for frying the fish
1	tsp light cream (optional)

♪   Wash and clean the fish pieces. Rub with turmeric and salt. Keep aside for 20 minutes. Heat 2 tbsp oil. Shallow fry the fish pieces till golden on both sides. Remove and keep aside.

♪   Now heat 1 more tbsp oil for cooking.

♪   Temper the oil with methi seeds, hing and bay leaves. The spices will sizzle in around 60–90 seconds. Then add the pureed tomato and green chilli. At medium heat fry the tomato for 4–5 minutes. There will be some sputtering as the tomato puree thickens, so use a lid or some kind of cover.

♪   When you see that there is no raw smell from the tomatoes and there is oil seeping out from the edges, add the ginger paste. Fry for a minute. Now add the cumin powder. Add around 1 tbsp water and fry the masala, scraping the sides for the next minute or so.

♪   Add about 1 cup warm water, salt to taste and let the gravy simmer till it comes to a boil. Add the fish pieces and let the gravy boil for about 2–3 minutes till the consistency is what you want. It should not be too liquid but should not dry up either. Add the sugar if you find the gravy too tangy for your taste.

♪   Add 1 tsp light cream and switch off the heat. Garnish with fresh coriander leaves if you wish.

DOI MAACHH
Fish in yoghurt sauce

Doi maachh or fish in yoghurt sauce is a typical Bengali dish which is light, easy to prepare and yet is a favourite as a dish you could serve your guests on those special occasions. I make this with rohu (a freshwater fish from the carp family), which I procure from my Bangladeshi fish seller. You can also try it with other fresh water fish. Salmon should also be a good bet. If the fish is very fresh and firm as it is back home, my Ma or Ma-in law does this without frying the fish. I, however, always lightly fry the fish. To make the gravy richer I sometimes add cashew paste which makes it taste heavenly. The cashew is not used in traditional Bengali recipes, so you can omit the cashews altogether if you want.

The doi maachh tastes best when eaten with white rice or pulao. And yes, do not forget to use your fingers. Fish needs a human touch and people who debone their fish with a fork, spoon and knife are missing out on half the fun.

6 pieces fish	**Whole garam masala**
2 cups chopped onion	5–6 green cardamom
2–3 tsp ginger paste	5–6 cloves
½ cup thick yoghurt	3 bay leaves
2 tsp turmeric powder	1" cinnamon stick
½ tsp Kashmiri mirch powder	
4 green chillies made into a	Salt to taste
paste + 4 cut in slits (adjust	1 tsp sugar
to your taste)	4 tbsp vegetable oil for frying
2 tbsp cashew soaked in	the fish. 2 tbsp for gravy.
water (optional)	1 tsp for frying the onion.
	Garnish – golden raisins if
	desired

♪ Clean the fish pieces and lightly rub with salt and a tsp turmeric. Keep aside for half an hour.

♪ Heat 1 tbsp oil. Fry onion for 5–6 minutes till they are soft and slightly browning. Cool and make a paste of fried onion, cashew and 4 green chillies together, with a splash of water.

ß Heat 4 tbsp oil in kadhai/frying pan. When the oil is sufficiently hot, gently add the fish and shallow fry at medium heat till light golden. Take out the fish with a slotted spoon and keep aside.

ß In a bowl, add yoghurt and about 1/3 cup water and beat till smooth in consistency. Add to this 2 tsp ginger paste, 2 tbsp onion paste you made, Kashmiri mirch and turmeric powder.

ß Heat 2 tbsp oil now for cooking the gravy. Once the oil is hot add the coarsely pounded whole garam masala.

ß When the masala starts sputtering, add the remaining onion paste. Add sugar and fry the onion paste till the oil separates. Add about 1 tsp ginger paste and the whole green chillies and sauté well, for about 1 minute.

ß Now take the kadhai/frying pan off the heat and give a minute to cool. Add the beaten yoghurt and mix with the masala. If you add the yoghurt directly when the utensil is on the stove it may curdle.

ß Put the kadhai/frying pan on the stove. Cook at low heat for two minutes. Add salt as required. Add about 1 cup of water at this point. Depending on how much gravy you need you might need more or less water. Simmer on low heat till the gravy comes to a boil. This will take about 5 minutes. Taste and adjust.

ß Add the fried fish pieces. Let them simmer till the excess water dries off and the gravy is thick, smooth and coats all the fish pieces.

Note: the gravy will not dry off totally but will be thick and not watery. This should take about 2–3 minutes.

ß Garnish with raisins if you want. Finish with a tsp ghee.

Ghoti, Bangal and Ilish

When we hired the help of a Bangladeshi babysitter about two years ago, I had harboured much hope. The deal was that she would also cook a couple of dishes for us during the week. I was giddy with anticipation. Part of this stemmed from the fact that I have a very high esteem for Bangal ranna. If I hear a friend's third cousin's second wife is a Bangal, the first thing I say is, 'How lucky, she must be a great cook.'

This blind faith has seeped in from hearsay and concocted stories about brilliant cooks from the east of Bengal. So when I got a Bangal babysitter, I gave into all her demands in hope of fabulous 'Bangal' cooking.

'Bangal' is the colloquial term for people from East Bengal, now Bangladesh. 'Ghoti' is the local term for people from West Bengal. 'Ghoti' and 'Bangal' have major differences in opinion on fish, football and food but otherwise have a peaceful coexistence.

After my Bangal babysitter had settled down and was made comfortable, I gingerly nudged her about the cooking part of her deal. It had been two weeks and I didn't see her jumping to wield the khunti or cooking spoon. Let's start with something simple, I thought. I had got a whole head of cabbage from the grocer's that week so I suggested she make a bandhakopir ghonto. 'Ghonto ki hoy, didi?' she asked, oblivious. Now really, there is no easy explanation for a term like 'ghonto', but I did my best, a bit surprised that she did not know such a common Bengali dish.

The lady did not appear very interested in all that I said and continued looking out of the window at the tall trees beyond. 'I can make a bhaji,' she said finally. Maybe they call ghonto a bhaji in Bangladesh, I thought.

The bhaji she concocted was a simple cabbage stir-fry with loads of green chilli, very, very hot but nowhere in the neighbourhood of a ghonto. This happened with most of the other veggies we brought home. Be it bitter-gourd, phulkopi or green beans, she always converted it into a bhaji. Then one day when I finally asked her if she could make anything different, she made a 'bhorta'. Thus it went, alternating between a bharta and a bhaji, the spicy hotness being the sole reliable factor in all her cooking.

When asked for fancier renditions like biryani or chaap or even pakoras, she proclaimed that back home it was her cook who made all this stuff and she was a 'working woman' who did not do much cooking. I kept my mouth shut and ate infinite loops of bharta, unprotesting.

If I hadn't had very strong faith in Bangal cooking (supported by several lunches and dinners at Bangladeshi and Bangal homes, including that of my in-laws') I would have seriously started doubting the Bangal ranna legend.

But the ilish beguner jhol that I will talk about now is so delicious that in spite of this episode, I still grovel at the feet of superb Bangal ranna.

Till the age of sixteen I didn't know that ilish (hilsa) could taste so good in a simple light jhol (a soupy gravy). Ma never made this particular preparation of ilish, it was always ilish bhaja (fried hilsa), ilish bhaape (steamed hilsa) or shorshe ilish (hilsa in mustard sauce) at home during the monsoon, the ilish season.

Years ago, it was on the day of Saraswati Pujo that I first tasted this different ilish dish. In our home (as in most Ghoti

Bengali homes), Saraswati Pujo was not only a vegetarian day, but a day on which you ate khichuri, bhaja, labra, chaatni and such. I was a teenager who didn't like her khichuri and to add insult to injury, this one was served without even an omelette. The day didn't hold much prospect of joy for me until my friend called and invited me over for lunch. I wasn't too enthusiastic about the food, assuming it would be the same fare, but the lure of her latest Sidney Sheldon acquisition pulled me along.

Come lunch time the table was laid and we sat. There were barely three covered serving bowls on the dining table and I felt forlorn, till her mom started serving. There was white rice, dal, aloo bhaja and an ilisher jhol.

'How can you eat fish on Saraswati Pujo?' I asked, aghast.

'Bangals have a tradition of eating ilish on Saraswati Pujo, and if it is jora ilish (a hilsa pair) all the better,' said the friend's mom. Wow, Bangals are such intelligent people. I must marry one of this species, I decided.

And then I saw ilish with all that begun, an ilish beguner jhol – hilsa in a light gravy with eggplant. I was skeptical, ilish being one fish that was not cooked with vegetables in our home, and then I took my first mouthful. The simplicity of the curry bursting with the flavour of soft brinjal, the taste of the hilsa and the mustard oil was too much for me. It was absolutely delicious; it shifted ilish's position from a special fish you would respect to a homely fish you could love.

I have been in love with this dish ever since. My in-laws, being Bangal, make this exactly the same way and now when I get ilish I make this for a light lunch. This is served with white rice for a homely meal and has no trappings to make it fancy, except the fresh light taste.

ILISH BEGUNER JHOL
Hilsa cooked in light gravy with eggplant

4–5	pieces hilsa cut in steak size pieces, washed and cleaned of scales.	5–6	green chilli slit
		1½	tsp turmeric powder
			Salt to taste
8	pieces of eggplant (chopped lengthwise in lengths of 3")	2	tbsp mustard oil for frying the fish + ½ tbsp more for gravy
½	tsp kalo jeere		

♪ Wash and clean the pieces of hilsa. Pat dry and smear with ½ tsp turmeric and salt. Keep aside for 15–20 minutes.

♪ Heat mustard oil to smoking in a kadhai.

♪ Gently slide the fish pieces into the hot oil. Fry them to a light golden brown on both sides. Remove with a slotted spoon.

Hint: Sometimes I sprinkle a little turmeric powder on the hot oil and then slide in the fish to reduce the splatter.

♪ Temper the remaining oil with kalonji and green chilli.

♪ Once the spices pop, add the eggplant. Sauté the eggplant with a little turmeric till it is lightly browned and soft.

♪ Add 1–1½ cups of water. Add salt and turmeric and cook till the eggplants soften. Sometimes I add a little coriander powder, but not often. Add the fish pieces and cook for 2–3 minutes.

♪ The gravy will be light and soupy and tastes delicious with white rice.

MAACHHER KAALIA WITH A TWIST
Fish kaalia

The kaalia is a jazzed-up fish curry with or without vegetables and perfect for a home lunch as well as for a Bengali meal in dinner jackets. While the maachher jhol is a lighter, soupy, stew kind of dish, the kaalia is a richer version with a surfeit of whole spices and onion and garlic. I remember Ma using phulkopi or cauliflower in this dish during winter. Many people prefer to call it maachh diye aloo phulkopi and reserve the word kaalia for a similar fish curry with only potatoes. Vegetables were seasonal and it was impossible to find a head of cauliflower in the summer days so potatoes were the mainstay. I have added cauliflower in this dish and I love this addition, but for a true-blue kaalia you can skip the cauliflower and continue with the recipe.

The day after a Bengali wedding, a rich, jewel-toned kaalia like this would usually be on the lunch menu to complement Ustad Bismillah Khan's shehnai on the loudspeaker.

You can use this recipe as a base and play around to find that taste or the taste that best suits you.

4 steak size pieces of fish (rohu/katla/tilapia) cleaned and with scales removed.	**For the paste:**
	½ cup chopped onion
	2 regular clove of garlic
	2 hot Indian green chilli
1 potato chopped in quarters	1 tbsp fresh grated ginger (about a 2" knob)
6–8 large-ish cauliflower florets, each 2" length (optional)	1 juicy red tomato chopped or pureed

For tempering:

1   bay leaf

2   cardamom

½ tsp loosely packed cumin
    seeds

1" cinnamon stick

Other masala:

  1   tsp cumin powder

  ½ tsp coriander powder

  1   tsp red chilli powder/
      Kashmiri mirch powder

1½ tsp turmeric powder

¼   tsp garam masala

½ tsp sugar

    Salt to taste

    Mustard oil – enough for
    frying fish and 3 tbsp for
    gravy. Instead of deep
    frying, I usually try to
    shallow fry the fish in
    3 tbsp oil

½ tsp ghee

- Clean the fish pieces. Rub with salt and ½ tsp turmeric. Shallow fry fish to a golden yellow, remove and then continue to make the gravy.

- Heat 2 tbsp oil. Fry the potato pieces and cauliflower florets with about ½ tsp turmeric and a sprinkle of salt till they are golden colour. Remove with a slotted spoon and keep aside.

- Add 1 more tbsp oil in the same pan. When the oil is hot, temper it with the ingredients for tempering. Let the spices sizzle and sputter and flavour the oil.

- Make the onion, garlic and chilli paste and add to oil. Sprinkle sugar and fry for 4–5 minutes or more till the paste starts caramelizing.

- Add the fresh, grated ginger and the chopped tomato. Raise the heat and fry till the tomato turns into a pulp. Sprinkle water and a little salt and continue cooking the tomato till it is reduced to a thick red gooey mass and oil starts seeping from the edges. This takes around 7–8 minutes.

᠔ Make a paste of the cumin powder, coriander powder, remaining turmeric powder and the red chilli powder with a tsp water. Add this masala paste to the above and fry the masala for 2 to 3 more minutes.

᠔ Next, add the potato and cauliflower, sautéing for about 2 minutes.

᠔ Add about 2 cups of warm water and mix well. Add salt and cover the pan. Let the vegetables cook.

᠔ Remove the cover and check the gravy for taste and consistency. Once the veggies are done add the fried pieces of fish and let the gravy simmer for 2–3 minutes. Reduce the gravy if you think it is a bit watery.

᠔ Finish with ghee and garam masala. Switch off the heat and keep covered until you serve it warm with fluffy white rice.

Variations: To make a jhol instead of a kaalia with this recipe, temper the oil with 1 tsp cumin, 1 bay leaf and a pinch of hing. Skip the onion and garlic and continue with ginger and tomatoes. Add more water if you want the gravy runnier. Enjoy with white rice and a lemon wedge on the side.

Lobsters in Maine

'Enough. I have had enough of this!' I declared. 'I cannot take this any more.' I was panting, slightly out of breath, bored even. What little remained of my mammary glands – after serving dinner on demand to two offspring – heaved sadly under the satiny ruffled top.

The H-man merely looked up from his plate with his 'not again' look and said, 'But it is you who wanted this.'

I could have said 'Maine mangi thi dhulai aur tune di hathon ki jalan' but it wouldn't have made sense. Because this wasn't about detergents or B-grade movies, this was about lobsters or rather too much of them.

A couple of summers ago we were up in Maine for a short vacation. Maine has a beautiful rockbound coast along the Atlantic Ocean, dotted with lighthouses, bays and thousands of offshore islands. Inland, there are forests and mountains with their sweeping slopes rushing to meet the sea. Normal people go there for relaxed vacations by the jade-blue waters of the bay.

I, however, had my priorities set right. Maine, with all its natural beauty, meant only one thing to me: lobsters. In the weeks leading to our vacation, I scoured enough websites to become a master of the restaurants of Bar Harbor, the town in Maine where we would be spending the next few days. I had made my lists, kept backups, diligently memorized each and every review on Trip Advisor and dreamed of sunny lobster-filled days.

I did not care to check the temperature, the precipitation level or the ensuing wind speed. I mean, who does that? Summer is supposed to be hot. So we drove up to Maine in late August with armloads of floral shorts and sleeveless tees and almost froze. The whale watching required jackets and pneumonia-proof souls. We had neither.

'You should have watched the weather. Pure common sense,' the H-man said gruffly.

'You are the one always watching Weather Channel,' I retorted.

H-man was clearly irritated and freezing in his shorts, and

snapped, 'And you Food Network. Your head is so full of butter and sugar from Paula Deen's Home Cooking that you forgot the umbrella when we went to Disney in 2009.'

'And remember in 1999 when we went to California, you forgot the raincoats.'

Thus we continued, going back to 1974.

Honestly, I couldn't care less about the weather. I had my lobsters. The lobster sautéed with parsley and butter at Rupunini, a restaurant that enticed me as much with its name as its butter lobsters; the lobster crêpes at Maggies scales; the steamed lobster at... it went on and on for lunch, dinner and snacks for three consecutive days even as we shivered and pulled our sparse clothes tight around us.

Until I could take no more.

'I know I wanted lobster, but does it always have to be this way? With butter and herbs or with herbs and butter? Such beautiful, succulent, fresh lobster meat and no one could think of anything other than sautéing it in butter?' I moaned.

The H-man rolled his eyes and tried to look away from the throngs of people waiting for a table at the bustling restaurant with the best lobster in town.

'How good would this have tasted in a malaikari? The silky coconut milk gravy would have complemented the juicy meat. The whole spices would have lent so many flavours. It would be, you know what they say, full-bodied. And served with some white rice, it would have been nothing less than ethereal,' I whined.

'The Return of the Bong,' the H–man muttered under his breath. Taraan–taraan, I could hear the music.

PRAWN MALAIKARI
Prawn cooked in coconut milk the Bengali way

250 gms prawns of the larger size, get fresh ones, with the heads on. This comes to almost 12 prawns	**Whole spices for tempering:**
	2 small bay leaves
	2 elaichi
	4 cloves
3–4 tbsp onion paste from a small onion	1" cinnamon stick
1 large clove of garlic chopped	½ tsp red chilli powder
1 tsp full ginger paste	1 tsp turmeric powder
4 slit green chillies	Salt to taste
1 cup thinned coconut milk	½ tsp sugar
	2 tbsp vegetable oil

🍴 Clean the prawns and mix with ½ tsp turmeric and salt and keep aside for about ½ an hour. Meanwhile, grind the onion to a paste. If your onion paste tends to get bitter, boil or fry the onion and then make a paste.

🍴 Heat 1 tbsp oil in frying pan.

🍴 Lightly fry the prawns so that they turn golden in colour, do not deep fry like other fish. As soon as the prawns turn a pale golden take them out and put them on a paper towel.

🍴 Heat 1 more tbsp oil and add the chopped garlic. As soon as the fragrance of the garlic rises, take the garlic out from the oil so that the oil is now garlic flavoured. This will happen in about 30-60 seconds. Take care that the garlic does not burn.

- Add bay leaf, clove and cinnamon. Slightly bruise the elaichi with a pestle and add that too. Add the sugar. It will caramelize in a minute.

- Add the onion paste next. Continue frying the onion till it turns brown and the oil separates from the paste. This takes about 4 minutes. Add the green chillies and ginger paste and cook the masala. This will take another 2 minutes.

- Stir and add the coconut milk. Add a little water (about ½ cup) and mix well.

- Add the red chilli powder, turmeric powder and salt. Mix well. Let the gravy simmer at medium heat and come to a boil. When you see the gravy bubbling, add the fried prawns. Cook on low heat for some more time till the gravy thickens and acquires a creamy consistency.

- Serve with white rice or yellow pulao.

CHINGRI MAACHHER DUM
Prawn and potatoes cooked in rich gravy

This dum is a dish in which the prawns are cooked on low heat along with the spices. The method of cooking is called 'dum'. The slow cooking at low heat makes this dish rich in flavours. I add potatoes to this dish as I love them, but I also think that they add a nice texture to this dish. To pretty this dish up for a party you can garnish it with fried onions. The part I like best about this dish is it is super easy and is done quickly even with the 'slow cooking at low heat' deal. Believe me.

10–12 medium to large sized shrimp/prawn, shelled and deveined	¼ cup thick yoghurt
	1 tsp turmeric powder
	1 tsp red chilli powder
4–5 small round potatoes or 2 large chopped in quarters	¼ tsp garam masala powder
1 medium sized onion, chopped	**For tempering:**
	2 bay leaves
2 heaped tsp ginger garlic paste	2 red chillies
	½ tsp sugar
2 green chillies	Salt to taste
	2 tbsp vegetable oil

𝄡 Put potatoes to boil and cook till they are fork-tender. Once they are done, cool and peel jackets.

𝄡 Heat 1 tsp oil in a heavy bottomed pan. Fry the chopped onion till it is soft and turns deep purple with a brownish tinge. Cool and put the fried onion in a blender jar. Add yoghurt and green chillies. Make a thick paste with little or no water.

𝄡 Put the shrimp and the boiled potatoes in a big bowl. Prick the potatoes with a fork. Add the onion-yoghurt-chilli paste, the ginger-garlic paste, turmeric powder, red chilli powder, salt to taste and toss so that everything is well coated with the masala. Keep aside for 30 minutes or more.

𝄡 Heat the rest of the oil. Temper the oil with bay leaf and dry red chilli. Add the sugar and let it brown a little.

𝄡 Next, add the marinated shrimp and potatoes along with the masala. Lower the heat and sauté for a minute, tossing everything together. Cover the pan and let the shrimp and potatoes cook at a very low heat. Once the masala is cooked (you will see oil surfacing at this point) open the cover and add about ½ cup warm water. Adjust for salt and sugar. Cover and keep cooking at low heat till the prawn and potatoes are done and the gravy is thick and clingy. Prawns get cooked fast and the dish will be done in 12–15 minutes even at low heat.

♪ Switch off the heat, sprinkle the garam masala, cover and let it sit for 30 minutes to blend in all the flavours. Warm and serve with white rice, pulao or even naan. It is superbly delicious.

The Kalo Jeere Tales

Kalo jeere in Bengali, kalonji in Hindi and Nigella in English is used in India and the Middle East as a spice and condiment and occasionally in Europe as both a pepper substitute and a spice. It is widely used in Indian cuisines for its smoky, pungent aroma.

In Bengali cuisine, it is almost as popular as paanch-phoron and used for tempering vegetable dishes, dals, fish curries and some chutneys. It is one of the five ingredients in paanch-phoron. It is also added to the dough while making nimki . The flavour within the seed is enhanced after it is baked, toasted or fried in a small amount of oil or the juices of foods.

These small, matte-black grains with a rough surface and an oily white interior are used in Indian medicine as a carminative and stimulant against indigestion and bowel complaints.

If I am talking about fish and I don't tell you about Bengali weddings, it wouldn't be fair to the fish.

Unlike their opulent Punjabi counterpart, Bengali weddings have no ladies' sangeet, no mehndi, no dancing and not even a single track of 'Munni Badnaam Hui' playing on the loudspeaker; instead there is the soulful shehnai, fat stalks of tube roses, crisp dhuti, food and of course, fish.

Bengali weddings are subtle and subdued, a lot like a black and white Satyajit Ray movie compared to a Karan Johar blockbuster.

'And you didn't even kiss after the wedding? Not even at the dance?' my friend's eleven-year-old daughter gasps.

'Yeah, tough luck kiddo,' I say. 'And by the way, what dance?'

Of my own wedding I have no glamorous memories. *DDLJ* came later and I have no regrets. I had spent so much energy making sure that I was getting married to the guy I wanted that by the end of it I just wanted the whole thing to be over and done with. Also, I had only two weeks of leave.

In between running to the tailor for blouse fitting sessions and convincing the husband-to-be that even in a Bengali marriage, I really, really needed a ring, I did not pay much attention to the rituals that I might have to face.

After all, I had seen enough, I told myself. It was not in vain that I spent five whole days just before my Class 12 pre-test being a part of my Chhoto Mama's wedding. I had spent hours trying to help with the tattwa – a gift of material things like sweets, spices, clothes, utensils sent to the bride's house and had been awed by the huge rohu with a bejewelled nose ring sent for gaaye holud, a ceremony which precedes the main event and involves applying paste of turmeric to the bride and groom. The most exciting part of this event is the gifts sent to the bride which almost always involves a huge fish.

So at my confident best, I was at the bank locker with Ma two days before my own wedding. Ma was appraising her boxes of jewellery and deciding which one of them would go with her cream and gold-trimmed Benarasi when my slightly older cousin said 'You might have to hold a live fish when you first step into your in-law's house, you know?'

I can still see myself in that tiny room, with sick greyish blue safe deposit boxes towering high, a fluorescent bulb shedding light and making the whole thing look like a prison cell. I looked at her, my jaws wide open in a very un-bridely manner. 'Whaaat?' I said.

'It is a ritual. New brides hold on to slippery live eels with all their might to prove that they are efficient managers...' she said. '... of slippery eels,' she smirked.

My jaw almost touched ground.

I was not an animal lover. To actually hold a live, slippery fish in your hands, especially when draped in a nine yard Benarasi saree was not my idea of entertainment.

The whole thing bothered me so much that I could not even concentrate on the fish fry that the caterers had sent as samples the day before. In hindsight that wasn't the best thing to do because on my own wedding day I could eat nothing of the wedding feast and could only chew on my nails when every other guest made it a point to say the fish fry was really great. To make matters worse, in my ensuing nervousness I had actually picked up the wrong wedding blouse from the tailor's, a size so small that I could barely breathe, forget eat, in it.

Sitting in front of the sacred wedding fire, I was so deathly pale, that the H-man whispered, 'Are you okay?'

Unable to contain myself, I let out a sigh. There was a pop and a button flew into the leaping holy fire.

'It can only get better.' I finally breathed easy.

The next day when I set foot in my in-laws' house after three hours of travelling on really bad roads, with stops for an amazing egg tadka at a roadside dhaba and totally hyped lyangcha in Shaktigarh, I had all but forgotten about the fish ceremony.

It seems my mother-in-law had too. Amidst the commotion and the conch shells, when I quietly whispered to her, asking if we might just skip the fish this time, she said, 'Definitely! We can have dim kosha instead.'

I knew I was in good company here. A mother-in-law who served a dazzling dim kosha, a sister-in-law who ate phuchka with as much eagerness as you might want and a husband who hated fish with gusto.

Dinner wasn't going to be easy with the H-man lighting a dozen incense sticks for every fish I fried. Sai Agarbatti Inc. was going to do booming business. Time to get the bird, I said.

Get Together for Dinner

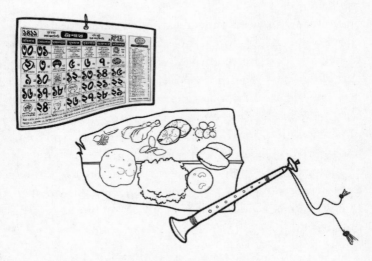

Dinner for a Bong goes beyond fish.
Depending on which came first, it can be an egg or
a chicken.

By the time Wednesday evening arrives I am totally uninspired about dinner. Cook in or take out? McDonald's or Domino's? Nazrul or Rabindranath? Satyajit Ray or Mrinal Sen? Satin thongs or cotton florals? Dimer jhol or dim kosha?

A Bong Mom has too many decisions to take and I totally empathize with parents who wait at a McDonald's drive-through or order pepperoni pizza from Domino's.

It is late in the evening and I have dropped my oldest at her taekwondo and ferried the youngest to the Mommy & Me play class. Most evenings, I don the role of a driver and zip around our small town between piano classes, swimming and hard-hitting martial art studios. You will know my kind: frazzled hair, glazed look and tattered capris. Yes, I am the official working mom cum chauffeur cum cook around here. My own mother doubts my multiple personality disorder and lives in eternal fear of her granddaughters not being well fed.

As I sit in the play area watching my little one confidently climb the slide all by herself, and think of dinner, I am just one phone call away from a Domino's half cheese, half onion and jalapeno pizza.

'What have you cooked for dinner?' Ma asks when she calls. She is an early riser and food is always the first thing on her mind.

'Umm, nothing yet. Maybe pizza.'

'Pizza? You want to feed the kids pizza for dinner? You know what they said in *Bartaman* yesterday?'

'What?' I ask reluctantly, not in the least interested in the Bengali daily's views on a flat piece of dough.

'Children in America are less intelligent because they eat so much pizza. No wonder none of them gets through IIT,' Ma proclaims confidently. 'Make some machher jhol and give it to them with gorom-gorom bhaat. They should eat fish and rice at least once a day. Basu jethi's grandson eats rice all three times and he is doing so well in school. I don't know why you think eating rice makes one fat. Carb-carb, you keep saying. Did you eat rice today? See, that is why you have no energy to cook now. Eat well and then exercise. How many times do I have to tell you this?'

'Are you doing the pranayam?' Baba's voice is distant. 'You can even do it at office, right in front of your computer. Close your eyes and concentrate and then breathe in-out, in-out.'

He must be kidding, I think. But no, my parents are dead serious.

It is not easy for me to set a home-cooked dinner on the table every evening. But goaded by my mother, I like to think that I am the kind of person who believes in simple meals cooked at home, a mother akin to Reema Lagoo in *Maine Pyaar Kiya*. I feel the need to do it more for my daughters than anyone else. I know that if I can give them the confidence of a warm kitchen and a bite of ginger in their dal, I will have set them up for life. I can instill in them respect for delicious, healthy food. In this journey I can also tell them who they are, where they came from and where they belong. Through the parade of spices in my kitchen I can talk to them about my dida, their didun, their thammi – and I hope they will talk about me one day in a similar fashion, in their own warm kitchens.

After much deliberation, I settle on dim kosha for the night. Eggs have a permanent place in my refrigerator, much like onion and garlic have a permanent residence in a wicker basket on the counter. The recipe is my ma-in-law's. Sometimes when my friends ask, 'What clinched your decision to marry the H-man?' I say it is my Ma-in-law's dim kosha. I cannot say for sure if it really clinched the deal but it did reduce my decision-making time by at least thirty seconds. After all, a guy who has been brought up on such good food cannot be a bummer.

The first time I had my Ma-in-law's dim kosha, the spiciness of the chilli hit me hard. There was nothing subtle about the thick gravy clinging to the eggs. It was bold, red and fiery and said in a loud voice 'take me or leave me'. It was Subhash Ghai in full blast.

I was in my mid-twenties, still undecided about marriage. That this petite lady with the hard-hitting dim kosha would be my Ma-in-law was not yet on the cards. There was still confusion, uncertainty, hesitance towards a lifelong commitment. I was one amongst the many friends invited to the H-man's house for lunch that day. The house smelled of onion and garlic and heavy spices in oil, the kind of smell that titillates your hunger and urges you to shun social norms and head straight to the kitchen. Even now, with all the windows open and the jasmine-scented spring air blowing in, my in-laws' house smells the same – of food and an eagerness to share it. The Ma-in-law, with true maternal instinct, had probably got a hint of the future and served her best at that first meal. She urged us to eat more and not once did she ask after my own cooking skills.

My husband's mother learned most of her cooking from her own mother-in-law, who had emigrated from East Bengal during Partition. Her food is hardy, makes use of every bit of vegetable, spice and legume in the pantry and is very different from my mother's sweetish and delicate flavours. She makes an amazing pâté-like dish with the peels of green plantain which I would normally throw away; she grinds vegetables like colocasia and seasons it with mustard oil and green chilli and she makes a mutton curry so hot that your heart is set on fire.

When I spend a few days with her (as I do every year), I see her concoct amazing meals with a nonchalance that seems almost irreverent to a new cook. When we visit, she insists on cooking by herself, relegating the help to minor chores like cutting vegetables and grinding the masala. I must admit that it makes me a little nervous to see her go about her cooking in so relaxed a manner. While I fret, she pores over the morning *Anandabazar Patrika* with a cup of tea by her side, showing no sign of entering the kitchen. The fishmonger or the vegetable-seller shouting out his wares outside the gate around mid-morning functions as the signal for her to start the culinary day.

I love how that makes her scurry to lower a basket into the front garden from the kitchen verandah and shout out instructions. 'One kilo tyangra – good quality – my daughter-in-law is here,' she announces. The same dialogue is repeated for the vegetable-seller, irrespective of my like or dislike of the items purchased. She ignores my rolling eyes and pitches my presence as an excuse to haggle over a kilo of green papaya. Then the peeling, chopping and stirring begins.

I grow anxious as the clock ticks on and the ma-in-law gets started on yet another dish with pumpkin stalks. 'Totally unnecessary,' I mutter to myself. She, however, glides along calmly, immersed in the fresh greens like an artist in her creation, making bold strokes of khunti against the iron kadhai, unaware of the strict norms of time. Once the cooking is done, the multicourse lunch is laid out, late in the afternoon but brimming with several little dishes, each vying with the other for accolades. Ucche bhaja shimmering with drops of oil, a pastel yellow moong dal with cauliflowers, feisty topaz-coloured mustard shrimp steamed in pumpkin leaves, the small tyangra fish in spicy gravy and her famous egg curry. The food is hot, spicy, heavy on the oil and delicious. When I got married, I knew this was amongst the many leaps that I would have to take.

I took that leap, but never made dim-kosha myself. Not even after I got married, when I should have tried to cook everything my mother-in-law did and pose the eternal question to my husband: 'Who makes this better, me or your mother?' But I don't like competition, especially when there is a huge chance that I might lose by a big margin. Also, I was not used to so much chilli or oil in my dishes. Cooking in my in-laws' home is very different from my mother's. I try to attribute it to the Ghoti-Bangal difference, relying on stereotypes like 'Ghotis like their food sweet while Bangals are all for fiery curries'. But I also think cooking is a lot about who you are and what you want out of life. So my ma-in-law's food is always made with lots of onion-garlic and is deliciously spicy, while Ma's is low on oil and flavourful with a hint of spices.

So I stuck to my mother's slightly sweet egg curry, dimer dalna, for a long time. My husband, surprisingly, did not complain. And yet, whenever we visited his parents or they came to visit us, the first thing we wanted her to cook was dim kosha. She would make it with the regular poultry eggs, eggs from farm-raised hens, even large duck eggs. It always tasted the same – absolutely delicious.

A year ago, I caved in and made dim kosha. I want it on my blog, I said. The H-man gave me his version of the recipe, what he remembered of it from his childhood. Of course, I could have called the direct source, but I've asked her so many times that she probably thinks I make it every week. I took courage and a deep breath and fried the boiled eggs till their skin was crinkly and wrinkled. I had never done that, never fried boiled eggs to death. Then I added enough oil to feed a village and made a totally lip-smacking dim kosha. The H-man said it was perfect, the best he had ever eaten. I wasn't a new bride anymore, so I didn't really care about the praise.

Ma-in-law's Dim Kosha
Spicy egg curry

This dish can be made as hot as you like. My ma-in-law makes her red chilli powder from dried red chilli and uses it liberally in this dish. When cooking for the kids I tone it down and often skip the chilli powder altogether. You can also use fewer green chillies, depending on how hot they are. Kashmiri mirch lends a nice red colour to the dish minus the excess heat so you can use that instead.

The same goes for the oil. I use less oil and don't fry the eggs too much on days when I am trying to be healthy. It's enough if you lightly fry the eggs in order to get the golden colour.

4	eggs	1	tsp cumin powder
1	large potato, peeled and chopped lengthwise	½	tsp Kashmiri mirch
		½	tsp red chilli powder
1	cup chopped onion, preferably red onion	¼	tsp garam masala powder
		1	tsp turmeric powder
½	cup tomato puree		Salt to taste
1	tbsp freshly grated ginger	¼	tsp sugar
¼	tsp garlic paste	3	tbsp or more oil (vegetable or mustard)
6	green chillies slit		
½	tsp paanch-phoron		

- Boil and peel eggs. Score the eggs on the top with a knife, smear a little turmeric powder, salt and a little red chilli powder and keep aside. Fry chopped red onion till it is browning on the edges. Cool and make a paste. Puree a medium sized tomato to make ½ cup tomato puree. Grate ginger.

- Heat oil. Fry the eggs till they turn reddish orange and the skin starts crinkling. Remove and keep aside. Fry the potatoes till they take on a light golden colour. Remove and keep aside.

- Temper the oil with paanch-phoron.

- When you get the fragrance of spices, add the onion paste and fry for a minute. Add the tomato puree, grated ginger, garlic paste and slit green chilli. Add a little salt and fry the masala at medium heat, till you see the oil separating from the masala.

- Now add cumin powder, turmeric and Kashmiri mirch. Keep

frying the masala with a sprinkle of water. This stage is called 'kashano' in Bengali and 'bhuno' in Hindi. At low-medium heat you need to fry the spice paste till the masala is cooked and turns a deep red in colour. This takes about 20-25 minutes.

♪ Now add the potatoes and toss them well in all the spices. Add 1 cup warm water, raise the heat and let the gravy come to a simmer. Adjust for salt. Once the potatoes are cooked, put in the eggs. Add sugar and garam masala. Taste and adjust for spiciness, etc. When the oil has surfaced, switch off the heat. Serve with rice or roti.

The Bengali dinner is an affair that, if not as detailed as the lunch, is certainly far richer. Though Bengalis are primarily rice eating homo sapiens, about 80 per cent Bengali homes serve ruti at dinner. Along with ruti, there is usually a dry vegetable dish and a fish curry. Some days, there will be egg curry and on special occasions a mutton curry. In many homes, mutton is restricted to Sunday lunch and dinner.

Contrary to popular belief, Bengali Hindu Brahmins are not vegetarian and do eat meat. Historically, the only kind of meat Bengali Brahmins were known to eat is goat meat. Goat meat was offered to Goddess Kali and the meat then cooked without garlic and onion. This is called 'Maha Prasad'. Many puritan Brahmins would eat meat only on this day as it was thought to be sacred.

Chicken was considered foreign and therefore not cooked in the home of the yesteryear Bengali Brahmin. Even hen eggs weren't eaten and the Brahmins restricted themselves to duck eggs alone. Thankfully, I eat both.

The Chicken That Defines Home

Sometimes I get philosophical over dinner. I ask myself, why do I love food? Is it because it satisfies me, gives me sheer unadulterated pleasure? 'Pssst, get on with the onions, this can wait,' my inner voice admonishes. But I am beyond onions, deep in my attempt to discover the true meaning of food.

Why does one remember food? Why do you want to go back to the comfort of dal-chawal even when you have been introduced to the delights of sushi? Why does cooking and eating a certain dish open a floodgate of memories? Why do some foods remind you of homecoming like no other?

While a meal of aloo posto and musuri'r dal reminds me of the home in which I grew up, there are others which remind me of the home I made for myself. Dhone pata chicken, the H-man's trademark chicken, is one of the latter.

Because I had a 'love marriage', my friends often ask me, 'So what did you do when you were going around?' They obviously want to hear something really scandalous, but unfortunately I cannot say a single exciting thing that will spark their interest.

Eloping, satyagraha, karvachauth, family feud, Goa, Daman, Diu – none of these figures in my story. If you can overlook my choking on a small toothpick while eating crispy duck in Schezwan sauce at Peiping and the H-man giving me a hefty shove to save me, there wasn't an ounce of the bold and the beautiful in the affair.

I can hear the sighs in my friends' voices.

But I was a bhodro Bangali girl, not one of those 'fast Delhi kinds' in designer jeans I secretly admired, so even if I wanted to do something scandalous, at the most I could snip grass and eat peanuts in the grounds of Victoria Memorial. But then there was the question of hygiene and the scorching sun and not very comfortable sitting arrangements. So really, nothing exciting happened in my courtship.

Just as my friends are about to lose interest, I tell them, 'But we did eat a lot. If someone sticks with you through ketchup and tamarind water, that counts.'

In my case it was far more than that. I loved to eat, and especially to eat out. Ditto the H–man. He did not have the Bong reverence for ombol, acidity and ajwain. Instead, he ate everything from jhaalmuri on the street to bean toast at Flury's with equal enthusiasm. The only thing he had no fascination for was phuchka, which I adored.

That could have been a point of contention. But we managed to live with this difference. After all, there was more food to argue over.

If I remember correctly, we started off our relationship with chicken kobiraji, spiced chicken cutlets fried in batter served sloppily with onions, mustard, ketchup and cold coffee at the India Coffee House just opposite Presidency College. Surviving apathetic waiters in elaborate headgear and insipid cold coffee in grimy glasses, we found a common ground of interest.

On searing hot days, traipsing along the narrow book lanes of College Street, we found solace in the rose sherbet bobbing with jagged pieces of ice within the cool interiors of Paramount Sharbat. Paramount did not believe in air–

conditioners or ice machines or anything remotely modern. Large slabs of ice wrapped in burlap sack were crushed somewhere on the premises and the constant sound of hammer against ice made the perfect background score to sharbat sipping: thump, thump, thwack, clink. This was our song. And that piece that fell off the block and right next to the sewer was the ice that would make its way into our glasses. We did not care.

If we were in the Park Street area, it was impossible to ignore the egg chicken roll at Hot Kathi or Kusum. Standing at the busy corner, tearing off bits of waxed paper wrapped around the fat roll where succulent pieces of meat and slices of onion snuggled, that was the pinnacle of our ambition. Then there were the hot momos at Tibetan Delight off Elgin Road and pastries at Kookie Jar. If we had money, we ate Chinese at Peiping or moist chello kebab at Peter Cat. When we worked in Bangalore, we ate petal-soft appam and stew for breakfast at Koshy's, stood in long queues at MTR for dosa and uppittu, had endless conversations over ice cream at Corner House and blew up our first paychecks on pad thai at Taj West End.

And then, of course, there was dhone pata chicken.

The H-man cooked this every weekend in the rented house he shared with another guy while working in Bangalore. Now, the H-man is a cooking geek, a freak of nature, the kind who chops vegetables in equi-dimension and whose eggs boil just right every time. On his bad days he can turn into a kitchen Nazi and demand each cauliflower floret be measured with a vernier caliper but in those days, I was ignorant of this.

At that time, I lived as a paying guest and was at the

mercy of the PG aunty for my meals. Though I was secretly quite pleased with this deal, I would rant about my sorry state and limited choices of food. This always ensured an invitation for Sunday lunch to the H-man's house and every weekend I found myself at his doorstep, drawn all the way from Malleshwaram to Koramangala by the aroma of coriander-infused chicken.

This dish slowly became the pivot of our lives.

When we set up our first home, we would cook this dish almost twice a week. It was very different from any of the Bengali chicken dishes my Ma made, yet it was hardcore Bengali with its fragrant paanch-phoron and crackling red chillies. Cooked in a pressure cooker with lots and lots of fresh green coriander leaves, the dish filled the corners of our house with its fragrance.

I have made slight changes to this dish since then, depending on my mood and the day of the week. My husband was a bachelor when he first started cooking this. He did not have a food processor. He did not make a paste. Actually, he never makes pastes. He might crush something, a thwack with the back of a spoon, but never a paste. But I am fond of my nifty food processors. If you do not have a food processor, just chop, mince, thwack and cook. Those of you who do own one, proceed with the paste.

Dhone Pata Chicken
Chicken curry with coriander leaves

1 kg chicken, skin removed and cut in medium pieces	**For the marinade:**
	1 tsp garlic paste
	1 tsp ginger paste

½   tsp red chilli powder

½   tsp turmeric powder

1   tbsp lime juice

1   tsp mustard oil
    Salt

1   tbsp the coriander
    paste

To make the coriander paste:

1   cup fresh coriander leaves

6   fat cloves of garlic

1   tbsp chopped ginger

4   hot green chillies

4   cloves

¼   inch cinnamon stick

1   tsp black pepper powder

1   tbsp yoghurt

For tempering:

1½ tsp paanch-phoron

2   dry red chilli

For the gravy:

2   cups red onion, sliced thin

1   juicy tomato, chopped

2   cups fresh coriander leaves,
    chopped

2   tsp coriander powder

½   tsp Kashmiri mirch (or red
    chilli powder)

½   tsp turmeric powder

¼   tsp roasted and ground
    paanch-phoron
    Salt to taste

½   tsp sugar

3–4 tbsp vegetable/mustard oil

⌁ Make the coriander paste. Wash and clean the chicken and marinate with all the ingredients listed under 'marinade' (ginger, garlic paste, chilli and turmeric powder, lime juice, coriander paste, salt, oil) for at least 30 minutes.

⌁ Heat the oil in a pan. Temper the oil with paanch-phoron and dry red chilli. When you get the fragrance of the spices, add the onion. Fry the onion with sugar till it begins to brown at the edges, about 5 minutes . Add the tomato and sauté till raw smell is gone, about 6–8 minutes.

⌁ Add the coriander paste and fry for a few minutes. Sprinkle a little water if it is drying up. Add coriander powder and Kashmiri mirch. With a sprinkle of water, fry the masala till it has blended well with the other ingredients and you see oil seeping from the edges.

♪ Add the chicken and a sprinkle of turmeric. Sauté till the chicken turns a nice yellow and the oil is surfacing, about 20 minutes. Add chopped coriander leaves, salt to taste and about 2 cups of warm water. Sprinkle roasted-ground paanch-phoron. Cover the lid and let the chicken cook.

♪ Once it's done, garnish with fresh coriander leaves and serve. The gravy is usually light, deep green in colour and tastes best with rice, though it can be eaten on its own.

Doi Murgi
Chicken in a yoghurt sauce

This is a soothing, mellow, yoghurt-based chicken dish. My daughters adore it. My mother used to make this dish with whole garam masala, yoghurt and onion paste. But I romanticize risqué. So when a blog reader suggested the use of Kasoori methi in this dish, I went ahead and tried it out. Warmed between your palms, those crushed, dried leaves have a heady fragrance. After that addition, the dish no longer remains mellow – it becomes a risqué dish.

1 kg chicken, skin removed, cut into medium pieces	1 tbsp yoghurt
	Salt to taste
For the marinade:	**Whole spices for tempering:**
1 tbsp ginger paste	2" long and thin cinnamon stick
1 tsp garlic paste	
1 tsp coriander powder	5 cloves
1 tsp cumin powder	5 green cardamom
½ tsp garam masala	8–10 whole black peppercorns
½ tsp turmeric powder	

For the gravy:

2	cups chopped red onion
5	fat garlic cloves
1	heaped tbsp chopped ginger
2–3	green chilli, if desired
1	cup yoghurt
1	tbsp cashew
½	tbsp Kasoori methi

½	tsp Kashmiri mirch
½	tsp or more red chilli powder, depending on your taste
	Salt to taste
½	tsp sugar
3–4	tbsp vegetable oil

♪ Wash and clean chicken. Marinate the chicken for 30 minutes to an hour with all the ingredients listed .

♪ Heat oil in a heavy-bottomed pan. Temper the oil with the whole spices. Add chopped red onion and fry with sugar till onion is soft and browned at the edges, about 5–6 minutes. Make a paste of garlic, ginger and green chilli with a splash of water. Add this paste to the pan and sauté for 2 minutes, sprinkling water if necessary.

♪ Add the chicken pieces, shaking off any excess liquid, and fry till they are lightly browned. Cook for the next 20 minutes or so, with frequent stirring until you see excess water drying up and oil separating. If needed, add a tbsp oil. Now add Kasoori methi crushed between your palms, Kashmiri mirch and red chilli powder. Sauté for 1 minute.

♪ Prepare a smooth paste of cashew and thick yoghurt. To avoid yoghurt curdling, remove pan from heat and add the paste .Mix with the chicken pieces so that all the pieces are uniformly coated. Wait for a minute and then put the pan back on low heat.

♪ Let it cook on low heat for 2 minutes. Now raise the heat to medium. Add about 1 cup warm water, salt to taste, mix everything and let it simmer and come to a boil. Cover and cook till the chicken is done.

♪ Taste and adjust for seasonings. The gravy should not be too runny, but rather should cling to the chicken pieces. If you see that the gravy is watery, reduce it by removing the cover and letting the dish simmer. Serve with rice or roti.

MY OWN KANCHA LONKA MURGI
My own green chilli chicken

My biggest foodie regret till date is that I didn't get to eat at Oh! Calcutta the last time I was in Kolkata. I had planned to land at Netaji Subhas Chandra International Airport after a 21-hour long-haul flight, pass through serpentine lines of immigration, spend hours at the luggage carousel, lose a piece of luggage or two, report it to officials and then drive straight to Oh! Calcutta for a dinner that included kancha lonka murgi.

Alas, this didn't happen. My parents, the H-man's parents and their neighbour's nephews were waiting for us at the airport and they hijacked my plan and whisked me, the kids and the H-man away to feed us mochar ghonto, thorer-something, moong dal and maachher jhol. And this didn't stop at Day 1. It continued day after day, relentlessly. I shouted, kicked, cried myself hoarse until I could just about whisper the words 'kancha lonka murgi'. I ate at a lot of places on that trip, including Mainland China (which was just a hop away from Oh! Calcutta), but I didn't get a single chance to tear myself away from the clan to dine at my chosen destination.

'Why would you want to pay so much money to eat Bangali ranna at a restaurant?' my ma-in-law would ask incredulously.

'We can get biryani and reshmi kabab packed if you like.

But no restaurant can make an enchorer kofta better than your ma-in-law!' said the F-I-L.

Next time, I am not going to give anyone my itinerary. I am going to land and drive straight to Oh! Calcutta.

Until then, I have devised my own version of the kancha lonka murgi. It has turned out to be the best thing I have made in my kitchen and it is hot, hot, hot. The seven-year-old gulps it down with tumblers of water, but has never refused it. With loads of green chilli, this is a dish to look out for.

450 gm boneless chicken thigh cut into small bite-sized pieces

To make a paste:
1/3 cup coriander leaves
4–5 fat cloves of garlic (or 10 regular)
2 tbsp peeled and chopped ginger slices
6 green chillies
1 tsp lime juice
1 tsp mustard oil

Whole spices
2" stick cinnamon
4 green cardamom

1 cup thinly sliced onion
8 green chillies, slit at the tip
1 tsp minced ginger
Salt to taste
½ tsp sugar
2 tbsp vegetable or mustard oil

𝄑 Grind to a paste the green chilli, garlic, ginger and coriander leaves with a splash of water. To this, add the lime juice and mustard oil and make a smooth paste.

𝄑 Marinate the chicken with some salt and half this paste and set aside for an hour. Keep the rest of the paste aside.

𝄑 Heat the oil and temper with a stick of cinnamon and green cardamom. Add 6 slit green chillies and the ginger. Sauté for a minute and add the onion. Fry with a little sugar for 4–5 minutes until the onion turns golden-brown. Add the remaining paste and fry for 2 minutes.

♪ Add the chicken pieces to the frying pan and sauté them till they lose their raw colour. This takes about 6–8 minutes. Add salt to taste. Add a couple more green chillies and cover the pan. Let the chicken cook, stirring in between. Toss chicken nicely with the masala. Sprinkle some water if the chicken is sticking to the bottom of the pan, but don't add too much. In about 10–15 minutes, the chicken will turn brown and be cooked. The final result will be a dry, moist dish.

♪ Serve with a wedge of lime as an appetizer or a side of roti or pulao.

MA'S GOL MORICH MURGI
My mom's black pepper chicken

Ma used to call this her 'chicken roast'. She also used to cook the chicken in pure, homemade dawn-coloured ghee – ghee she would make at home after saving the cream from the milk for days. It was a l-o-n-g process. The aroma of her dish, therefore, is hard to beat. Sometimes I make ghee at home from organic butter, but mostly I use store-bought ghee for this dish and make the most of it.

I call this dish gol-morich chicken so as not to confuse it with a Western-style whole roasted chicken. No roasted chicken can come close to the delicious taste of this dish. It is also super easy and super quick and demands very few ingredients. All it needs is a good dose of freshly crushed black peppercorns. Yes, freshly ground – the kind that comes in a bottle won't do.

I usually cook this dry and serve it as an appetizer, but it also goes well with soft paratha or roti.

250 gm boneless chicken thigh pieces cut up

For the marinade:

1 tbsp ginger garlic paste (fresh-made is best)
½ tbsp black pepper powder, fresh made
1 tsp lime juice
Salt to taste
½ tsp oil/ghee

For frying:

1½ tsp ginger garlic paste
2 tsp black pepper powder
20 whole black peppercorns
2" stick (thin) cinnamon
Salt to taste
2 tsp vegetable oil
2 tsp ghee

For garnish:

½ a small onion, fried
Quarter of a lime

♪ Marinate the chicken pieces with all that is listed under 'marinade'. Leaving it overnight will get you the best results. If not, at least leave it for a couple of hours. Fry the onion and set aside to be used later as garnish.

♪ Heat the oil and ghee in a frying pan. Temper the hot oil with the whole peppercorns and cinnamon stick. The peppercorns will sizzle in a minute. Now add the pepper powder and the ginger-garlic paste. Fry the spices for 2 minutes at low-medium heat.

♪ Next, add the chicken pieces and toss with the spices. Raise the heat and fry the chicken pieces for the next 4–5 minutes till they lose the raw colour. Add salt to taste and cover the pan. Cover and let the chicken cook. Lift the cover and stir in between. Sprinkle some water if the chicken is sticking to the bottom of the pan, but be careful not to add too much water. In about 15 minutes the chicken will turn brown and be cooked. If you had not cut the chicken into small pieces, break it up now and toss nicely with the masala.

♪ Squeeze some lime juice on top and garnish with the fried onion. Serve it up. It is delicious.

Sunday Mutton Curry

When I was a child, Sundays were special. They still are, but back then this was the only day of the week when everyone had a holiday. Marked in red on the black digit calendar, Sunday was the day I waited for with great anticipation.

I would wake up on Sundays to the sound of a pressure cooker, its shrill whistle repeating itself in a steady rhythm, almost like a steam engine. I would look around, waiting for Ma to turn it off. Pressure cookers scared me. I was afraid it might burst but Ma let it hiss, switching off only after the whistle had gone off at least five or six times. With every whistle, the fragrance of what was cooking in its steel interiors would trace the room, trying to find its way out of the wide windows. By noon, when the sun was high up, the drapes tightly drawn, I would be sprawled on the sofa along with friends from the neighbourhood waiting for the Sunday morning episode of Spiderman on TV. Even as Spiderman saved the world, my mind wandered in anticipation of lunch.

Ma spent those mornings entirely in the kitchen, her cotton saree damp and turmeric-stained, smelling strongly of Sunday, of mutton curry. She did not prefer company there and shooed me away but with a sidelong glance I could see the fresh, marbled pieces of meat bought that very morning from the butcher shop. The meat was washed carefully in a steel dekchi and then dusted with salt, brilliant yellow turmeric, scarlet red chilli, dollops of white yoghurt and drizzles of mustard oil. Ma never really followed a set recipe for mangshor jhol; she added the masalas – cinnamon, cumin, ginger – without much thought, but through some deep seated instinct the Sunday mutton curry always revolved around the same core – a reddish gravy with large chunks of potatoes and fatty pieces of meat. And it always managed to taste the same.

For a few years in my childhood, we lived with my paternal grandparents who were strict Brahmins. So the only meat that was allowed in our home was goat meat – not chicken. If we wanted to eat chicken it was to be cooked out in the garden, which was quite a hassle. So Sunday lunch was almost always mutton curry-rice, an affair the family looked forward to. I wasn't very fond of goat meat then, but loved the gravy and the butter-soft potatoes. Sucking at the bones and pounding them hard on the plate to pull out the soft juicy marrow was my favourite activity during those meals. We ate with our fingers and sucked at bones which made clattering noises against the steel plate. The fragrance of the curry lingered on my fingers long after I had washed them with Dettol soap.

Now I am in a different country, on a different Sunday. I still try to continue the tradition of Sunday mutton curry. Only most Sundays it is chicken and not mutton but I try to stick to the same basic core of mangsho'r jhol. Soon after breakfast I start chopping onions, shedding copious amounts of tears in the process. I put fat cloves of pearly garlic and pieces of ginger in the blender and make my own ginger-garlic paste. I count out whole green cardamom and tiny black cloves on the kitchen counter to put in the hot oil. I take out a pack of curled brown cinnamon sticks and select one that is slender and firm.

Once I have finished with 'kashano', frying the meat till the oil resurfaces, I close the lid tightly on the pressure cooker. I am no longer afraid of this contraption. My Futura pressure cooker does not whistle either, it hisses mildly. With each hiss, the aroma of mangsho'r jhol reverberates through our home. Later I cook rice in the same cooker, the meat stock flavouring the rice.

Thus my Sunday afternoons are never a quiet affair but rich and passionate with mutton curry and rice, laughter and adda.

MANGSHO'R JHOL
Mutton curry

The taste of the mangsho'r jhol depends largely on the goat meat used. I was unaware of these technicalities before and had no idea that different cuts made the dish taste different. I am wiser now.

For most Indian curries, shoulder and the hind leg are the best sections to use. Tell your butcher that you want these cuts or nothing. I prefer goat meat pieces with at least some fat clinging to them. Those yield a ton of oil during kashano and I need to start with very little oil from my own supply. It is also my belief (unproven) that it makes the dish more delicious. If you are the kind that eats red meat but worries about the fat, ask your butcher to trim it away.

The recipe will work perfectly for both chicken and goat meat. But if you are cooking chicken, you will need a little more oil as poultry is much leaner than mutton.

1 kg mutton cut into medium-sized pieces	7–8 fat cloves of garlic (14–16 regular sized)
2 medium / 1 large potato	2 inch knob ginger

For the marinade:

5–6 hot green chillies

3 tbsp thick yoghurt

1 large juicy tomato finely chopped (optional)

1 tsp mustard oil

1 tsp vinegar or lime juice

1 tbsp cumin powder (Some days I use coriander instead of cumin, but never both together.)

1 tsp garlic paste

1 tsp ginger paste

Salt to taste

2 tsp red chilli powder, depending on your taste

1 tsp turmeric powder

Whole spices for tempering:

2 tsp turmeric powder

Salt to taste

5 green cardamom

1 tsp sugar

5 cloves

2–3 cups water

2" inch stick cinnamon

¼ tsp lime zest or a couple of lime leaves

2 bay leaves

Other ingredients:

Oil (3 tbsp for mutton and at least 5 tbsp for chicken)

3 cups roughly chopped red onion (approx. 3 large onions)

♪ Marinate the meat with the listed ingredients. For mutton it is better to marinate overnight, but for chicken a couple of hours will do.

♪ Heat 1 tbsp oil in a deep, heavy-bottomed pan. Add the onion and fry till it turns maroon and golden with deep brown edges, about 5 minutes. Add the garlic and ginger. Sauté for a couple more minutes. Cool and then grind the onion, ginger and garlic to a fine, smooth paste with the aid of little water.

Note: Traditionally, raw onion, garlic and ginger paste is used in this dish. I do this because raw onion paste sometimes tends to get bitter.

♪ Heat the rest of the oil in the same pan. Temper the oil with the whole spices. Next, add 1 tsp sugar and caramelize it. This gives a nice colour to the gravy.

♪ Add the onion, ginger and garlic paste from the blender and fry for about 3 minutes. Add the green chillies, roughly pounded. Add the chopped tomatoes if using. Fry till the tomato is all mushed up and you see the oil separating from the edges. This takes about 6–7 minutes. Add cumin powder, red chilli powder and turmeric powder, all mixed together in a tsp water and fry for 2–3 minutes.

♪ Add the meat pieces, shaking off any excess liquid, and fry till they are well coated with the masala. Raise the heat and let it cook uncovered for the next 20–25 minutes or so, with frequent stirring, until the water released from the meat starts drying up. At the end of this process you will see the oil separating.

♪ While the meat is cooking, in a separate pan, fry the peeled and quartered potatoes with a pinch of turmeric powder till they take on a nice golden colour.

♪ When you see the meat pieces are no longer raw and the oil has separated from the masala, transfer everything to a pressure cooker. Add about 2–3 cups of warm water, the fried potatoes, salt and mix everything well. Close the pressure cooker lid and cook at medium-high heat till meat is done. Chicken usually is done in 3–4 minutes at full pressure while mutton will take about 10–12 minutes. This timing is for the Futura pressure cooker, for other brands it might vary.

♪ Once you switch off the cooker, let it rest till the steam subsides. When you open the lid, you should see a red coloured gravy with a thin layer of oil floating on top. Add about ¼ tsp lime zest or lime leaf if you have one, and keep covered till you serve. This lends a beautiful flavour to the rich curry. Garnish with loads of chopped coriander leaves for a chicken curry. For a mutton curry, skip the coriander leaves. Serve with white rice, salad and a wedge of lime on the side.

MUTTON REZALA

Mutton rezala is a very fragrant stew that speaks volumes about Mughlai influence on Bengali cuisine. The best rezala in my time could be found at Sabir's in Kolkata. It was out of this world. Over the years, that taste has ebbed in its sharpness but I still remember my anticipation when Baba brought home biryani or paratha-rezala from Sabir's.

Over time I learned to live with the fact that rezala was one more unattainable thing from the past. It was a dish fit for nawabs who led a luxurious, sedate lifestyle and had no place in the modern world with its Pilates and Zumba and salads with feta cheese. Rezala must be slow-cooked on a charcoal fire, said Sabir's chef, and who has the time to do that now?

And then one day, I woke up bright and shiny and cooked rezala. Just like that. As the mutton cooked, its scent serenaded my home. Even the gods did not need their Sai Darshan agarbatti. The cinnamon-apple candle shut down in shame. The jasmine (if I had any that is) would have bowed its head to this ethereal aroma.

It was fragrant, the mutton tender and soaked with zafran, javetri, elaichi and laung, the gravy light but spicy. Basically it was everything I could ask for in a rezala. The flavour of this dish comes from the whole spices, cardamom, javetri and the magical drops of kewra water. Everyone who has tasted it loves it. And guess what? It is not even difficult to cook. Except for the charcoal fire of course, which I skipped.

2.5 kg mutton

To make paste:
4–5 cups roughly chopped
     red onion.
12   cloves garlic
2"   piece ginger
3   cups yoghurt in total,
     1 cup for the marinade and
     2 cups for later

To grind to a dry spice powder:
4   big black + 20 green
     cardamom
1   tbsp mace/javetri
10   clove
1   tbsp pepper powder

Whole spices for tempering:
5   bay leaves
15   red chillies. Do not crack the
     red chilli, use them whole
     as this brings you the smell
     of the spice without excess
     heat. Depending on your
     spice level, decrease or
     increase this quantity.

3–4 tsp whole black
     peppercorns
2   black + 10 green cardamom
15   clove
4–5 cinnamon sticks

For the gravy:
2   tsp ginger paste
2   tsp garlic paste
4   tbsp cashew soaked and
     then made into a paste
1   tsp kewra water (must-
     have for the fragrance)
2   tbsp milk
     A few strands of good
     quality saffron
1   tsp sugar
     Salt to taste
2   tbsp vegetable oil
1   tbsp ghee

꙳ Heat the oil. Fry the onion, garlic and ginger until the onion is soft and translucent. This takes about 5 minutes. Cool and make a paste. Add to this 1 cup yoghurt and blend well.

꙳ Traditional route: don't fry the onion, garlic and ginger; just make a paste directly.

꙳ Make dry spice powder. In a big, large-mouthed bowl add the washed and cleaned mutton pieces. Add the paste with yoghurt and the dry spice powder. Add salt to taste. Mix well. Let it rest for 2–3 hours or (if possible) overnight. Overnight is best as it lets the spices soak into the meat.

꙳ Heat 2 tbsp oil and 1 tbsp ghee in a heavy-bottomed, large pan. If the meat has some fat don't add too much oil to start with. In that case the meat will cook in its own fat.

꙳ Temper the oil with all the whole spices listed under 'tempering'. Add about ½ tsp sugar.

꙳ When the spices sizzle, add 2 tsp ginger paste and 2 tsp garlic paste and fry for couple of minutes.

꙳ Remove the meat pieces from the marinade, shaking off any excess liquid, and add them to the pan. Sauté the meat pieces till the raw pink colouring is gone. Some water will be released at this point and it will smell heavenly. It will take at least 20–25 minutes.

꙳ In a bowl, beat about 2 cups of yoghurt and cashew paste together. I also add a little sugar to the yoghurt so that there is no sourness. Lower the heat and add this, along with the remaining marinade, to the pan. Mix everything nicely. Add salt to taste.

꙳ Transfer everything to a pressure cooker. If you think that the liquid is not enough, add some water. Add a tsp Kewra water. Now close the lid and cook till the mutton is tender. The marinated goat meat usually takes about 10–12 minutes to cook at full pressure.

Note: if you do not have a pressure cooker, you can cook the meat in the pan but it will take about 45–60 minutes. You will also need to stir in between and add water if necessary to avoid having the meat stick to the bottom.

♪ In a small bowl, heat 2 tbsp milk and add a few strands of saffron. Once the meat is done and you can open the lid of the cooker, add the milk and saffron mix and close the lid again. Let it sit for 30 minutes and then serve with rice, biryani or naan.

MUTTON KOSHA
Slow-cooked spicy mutton

Mutton kosha is stuff that dreams are made of. Slow-cooked and snuggling in spices, the soft morsels of meat in burnt sienna gravy is the perfect dream girl. With the amount of time you spend cooking, it better be. I mean, if you've spent an hour cooking mutton you don't want it described as anything less than 'superbly, fantastically delicious' and that is exactly what this is.

The best mutton kosha is apparently found at Gol Bari, a restaurant at the five-point crossing in Shyambazar just across from where Netaji Subhas Chandra Bose rides his stallion amidst screaming state transport buses and honking cycle rickshaws. The restaurant is actually called New Punjabi Hotel but it is more famously known as Gol Bari because of the semi-circular façade of the building. Every time we took the bus from my Dida's house, which was further north, and passed the overcrowded 'paanch mathar mor' at Shyambazar, I looked out longingly for the familiar Kolkata landmark.

An earthenware pot of deep brown Gol Barir kosha

mangsho with a shimmering layer of oil on top, the fabled chutney and soft hand rolled rotis rarely entered my life. But it is a vision that I strive hard to recreate. I am almost there but not quite. Well, some things are best when we are 'almost' there rather than absolutely on the dot. This is one of them.

1 kg mutton

For garam masala:
8 green cardamom
8–10 cloves
2 ½" pieces mace/javetri
1" cinnamon stick
3 dry red chillies

To make a paste:
10 fat cloves garlic (20 regular)
3" piece ginger
5–6 green chillies

Marinade for mutton:
1 tbsp ginger-garlic-chilli paste (made from the above)
1 tbsp vinegar or lime juice
1 tsp mustard oil
  Salt to taste
1 tsp turmeric

Whole spices for tempering:
4 green cardamom
4 clove
1" cinnamon stick
2 bay leaves
1 dry red chilli

For gravy:
3 cup thinly sliced onion (approx. 3 large onions)
1 medium tomato, chopped
4 tsp yoghurt
1 heaped tsp cumin powder
1 heaped tsp coriander powder
2 heaped tsp red chilli powder
1 tsp turmeric powder
  Salt to taste
1 tsp sugar
3 tbsp vegetable oil

♪ Dry roast the spices listed for 'garam masala' and grind them to a fine powder. This is the masala that will be used in the mutton curry. Make a paste of garlic, ginger and green chillies with a splash of water. Marinate the mutton with everything listed under 'marinade' for 3–4 hours or overnight. If you are marinating only for a few hours, add a tbsp papaya paste to the marinade as tenderizer, else the mutton will take a long time to cook.

And then start cooking:

🎵 Heat the oil in a deep, heavy-bottomed pan. Add 1 tsp sugar and swirl the pan. In 1–2 minutes it will caramelize and turn a nice brown.

🎵 Temper the oil with the whole spices listed under 'tempering'. As soon as you get the fragrance of the spices, add the sliced onions. Fry for about 4 minutes till onion turns soft and starts browning at the edges. Then add the ginger+garlic +green chilli paste and fry for 2 minutes. Next, add the chopped tomato and fry till oil separates from the masala.

🎵 Meanwhile, in a small bowl, make a paste with yoghurt, cumin powder, coriander powder, turmeric powder, red chilli powder (adjust the latter according to your level) and the dry garam masala you made earlier. Lower the heat and add this masala paste. Fry for 1 minute at low heat.

🎵 Add the mutton and mix it nicely with the masala. Add salt, and at medium-high flame let the mutton cook in its own juice. Stir in between. This process is called 'kashano' and will take up to 30 minutes at medium heat.

🎵 Once you are done with the kashano the mutton will have lost its raw colouring. Now add about 2 cups of warm water, mix well and cover the pan. Cook the mutton in the covered pan itself. Remember to stir in between and add water if necessary. You can use a slow cooker if you have one and cook the mutton in it too.

🎵 Cook till the mutton is done. It will take nearly an hour for the mutton to be done to softness. Check for seasoning and adjust according to your taste. Enjoy this delicious kosha mutton with a fluffy pulao or roti.

♪ When I eat this mutton curry with rice, I like to squeeze a little
   lime juice on it and have sliced red onions as a side.

The Biryani Masala Tales

'Biryani masala,' whispered the javetri to the jaiphal. 'We are
going into a biryani masala- fine, fragrant, sensuous. We are
going to spice up those humans' everyday lives.'

I often alternate between biryani masala and garam masala
in my cooking, substituting one with the other as the situation
demands. No store-bought biryani masala serves this purpose,
though. The one I use is homemade and redolent with the
fragrance of javetri and jaiphal.

Dry roast 8–10 green cardamom, 8–10 cloves, 2" stick of
cinnamon, 1 small bay leaf, 5–6 small barks of mace/javetri, 2
tsp fennel seeds and 1 tsp carraway seeds/Shah jeera.

Put all of the above in a coffee grinder jar along with 1 tsp
nutmeg powder.

Grind to a smooth powder and store in an air-tight jar.

When I had finished cooking the perfect kosha mangsho,
sweating it out for an hour, Friend 1 called to tell me that
she was going on a detox cabbage broth diet. These diets
were a hobby for her, but this time her sister was getting
married in two months and my friend wanted to fit into a
size 2 backless choli. She wanted me to give her company.
'Please salt my broth,' she implored. I refused. I was not
even going for the wedding and had no teeny blouse sizes

to fit into. What was going to motivate me to eat boring broth?

Next in line was Friend 2. She had signed up for Zumba class. Her sister's engagement was only a month away. She would attend via Skype and desperately needed to fit onto the screen.

'You have to come with me to the class,' she wailed. 'I need a moral conscience. You could be my voice of reason.'

I wasn't too sure. I mean, on a good day I don't have enough reasons to even convince myself, let alone other people. But I trudged along with my two left feet. Dancing is not my forte, more so Latin dancing. But Zumba sounded exotic and illicit, like chocolate-dipped strawberries for lunch. I imagined graceful women with flaming red lips in swishing silks being twirled around by tall dark men with taut muscles. Instead in that fateful class, I found myself in a room with mirrors and neon lights, surrounded by women, all fit and flat, their slim legs encased in fitted black tights, their chests pulled back in black tank tops.

And then the beat started. It was pulsating, fast and made your heart jump. The instructor's firm belly shook and trembled and took on a life of its own. She jumped, cavorted and shouted 'Exhale, inhale, crunch your butts, hold, hold, hold!' The ladies in black followed on cue, graceful, swaying, their movements to the beat.

Having grown up on Bollywood tracks, I should have literally danced through this. But I am directionally challenged. While all the fit ladies in black went left, I in my faded tee and crumpled yoga pants went right. While they shook their slim waists in circles, I with the girth of Saroj

Khan shook my hips like Amitabh Bachchan. I wiggled and jiggled and sweated and panted.

After a month, Friend 1 lost two pounds and could struggle into her bling-bling sequined choli and Friend 2 managed to dump half a pound. I lost nothing but self-esteem. To celebrate, I made mutton kosha. Again. After all, I was the one who was going to miss out on the fabled wedding feast, the biyebarir bhoj.

The spicy mutton kosha and sticky pineapple chutney always remind me of weddings. Of lilting notes from the shehnai, the heady scent of jasmine garlands slightly crushed by heat, flatulence and perspiration mingled with Chanel 5 from Chor Bazar and rising above it all, the smell of fish fry and kosha mangsho.

This was weddings in the days before the caterer, when wedding food was cooked at the venue itself and there were no printed menus with misspelt names like 'Shubha weds Shubha' on the outside. Depending on whose son or daughter was getting married, my Thamma would start discussing the food soon after the flat rectangular wedding invitation with a dot of turmeric had been opened. There were folks in the extended family with a reputation for throwing lavish dinners, while some were known to be stingy even during their eldest daughter's wedding.

Coming from a generation that had seen several wars and riots and knew the uncertainty of possessions, my grandmother was very careful about the gifts she gave at these weddings. The monetary tag on the gift she chose would almost always be proportional to the quality of the food, which she made wild assumptions about. At times she fortified her assumptions with backstage stories from one of my father's distant uncles, Shona dadu, who came every Sunday evening bearing gossip about our distant relatives and eagerly shared them over cups of sweet hot tea.

Shona dadu slurped his tea straight from the saucer and swallowed in loud forceful gulps. He raised his dhoti above his knees, made himself comfortable and sat crosslegged on the couch. We sat around him expectantly. Ma and Kakima stood by the door, ready to bring more tea if needed. Shona dadu then went on to describe the five-star opulence of an impending wedding of Baba's third cousin. 'Ki arrangement korse, five star hotel keo har manaye dey,' he would declare in his heavy East Bengal accent.

Thamma would mentally calculate whether she could pass on a set of glass tumblers for such a five-star wedding and then ask Shona Dadu to get hold of the feast menu.

Due to her frail health, Thamma was not able to accompany us to many of these weddings. And the first thing she would ask when we returned late at night was what we were fed. 'Ki khawalo?' she would ask, her voice tinged with curiosity.

Puffed up radhabollobi, aloor dom and chholar dal garnished with tiny pieces of coconut, plump brown beguni, sweet saffron pulao, rui maachher kaalia and kosha mangsho were the staple at these weddings. There would be slices of greenish yellow kagji lebu (lime) with a pinch of salt on the side. To finish off, there would be a sticky chutney, papad and mishti. You could expect no less.

As much as I loved the glamour and food associated with these weddings, I also had a niggling fear of them. Due to some crazy, Freudian reason, I was always afraid of spilling the oily gravy of the mutton or the sticky goodness of the chutney on my best dress in those settings.

You see, during those days Bengali weddings were home-grown affairs with a multi-coloured pandal put up on the terrace or front lawn. The three-day-long wedding feast was cooked at home by the hired thakur and his entourage. Food was served on freshly washed banana leaves and water was served in 'khuri' – small earthenware pots, which sat eager to be knocked over at the slightest nudge. The whole ensemble sat atop long rickety wooden tables in a neat row. The wooden folding chairs placed on the uneven ground wobbled and shook if you so much as shifted your torso. It all needed a fine balance.

Eating dal, chaatni and kaalia off those shiny flat banana leaves was a tricky affair. One had to be fast and possess excellent motor skills to prevent any spillage. As the dishes arrived one after the other in huge brass buckets amidst mixed aromas and lots of chatter, I would work furiously with three fingers of my right hand, scooping, tearing the meat and putting morsels in my mouth. The servers were usually family and they made small talk, asking for Ma's choice of fish piece and whether I preferred mutton pieces with a meaty marrow. Ma never liked that I refused perfectly good fish at these weddings. 'Maachh ta nebe,' she would insist in a low but stern voice. Thrown in the mix were numerous aunts, the kakis and jethis resplendent in their silks and jewels, who asked random questions about math scores and darkening complexions. A moment's carelessness in that situation could cause serious damage.

By the time the crackling papad and chaatni arrived, there would be a delicious mess on my platter. The remains of chholar dal mixed with the heavy spices from the kosha mangsho and was sweetened with the chaatni. I would scoop it all up with pieces of papad and heave a sigh of relief. I had survived one more wedding feast.

It has been a long while since I attended a 'proper' Indian wedding. It has not been possible to match the wedding dates in India with scheduled time-offs here. With every heavy envelope embellished with the shiny gold letters of 'Shubho Bibaho' that has arrived, I have felt a pang for that fish fry lost, the radhabollobi that was not eaten.

Ideally, the 11 yards of tussar silk lying at the bottom of my suitcase or the slate blue dhakai that gathers dust should have deserved more of my sympathy. But I am more than relieved at the fact that I don't have to wear them. It is the food I miss the most, and the gossip afterwards. 'Chhee, the chilli fish tasted like leather. Only son's wedding and such ordinary food! And the pulao, did you see it was cooked in dalda? Remind me to take Digene when we reach home,' an aunt would say, wiping the last traces of mutton kosha oil from her fingers onto a checked cotton handkerchief.

I should not complain, though. To compensate for those evenings, Bengalis where I live celebrate every occasion marked on the calendar and a few that are not. Every birthday, anniversary, Halloween, Bijoya, Thanksgiving, Christmas and New Year is celebrated with as much food as only a wedding deserves. Large, tightly covered aluminium trays warm in the oven. Platters of crispy samosas are fried up and served along with wedges of cheese and an assortment of crackers. Rosogollas are made painstakingly and devoured with gusto.

Having anything healthy or non-Bengali on the menu is regarded as blasphemy. If it is Thanksgiving, the table is laid out with a whole turkey which the guests regard as lacking in taste, mashed potatoes which they itch to add mustard oil to, green beans which are completely ignored and then an onslaught of rice, bandhakopir ghonto, dal, maachher kaalia and pathar mangsho. On Christmas, we have roasted chicken, a pie or a pudding and then the full Bengali six-course meal. The pattern remains the same for every holiday.

It is not surprising that a bunch of people from similar backgrounds who have immigrated by choice for a better life get together every weekend to re-live the life they hurriedly left behind. I enjoy these parties, but when it's my turn to host the do – which comes about twice a year – a chill goes down my spine. In my decade-long existence in this country, I have learned the hard way that to feed Bengalis in the US is not an easy task. It takes years of practice, a well toned upper arm to stir pounds of meat, and shots of vodka to embark on that magnum project. I might be a food blogger and a hundred odd people might pop in to my blog and say that my 'Pui Chingri' is awesome but trust me, it does nothing to boost my confidence when it comes to cooking for the Bong party. I am in eternal fear of the competent female Bongs whose expectations of such parties run as high as their plunging necklines scoop low. I admire them. After all, they are the pioneers who replicated mochar ghonto with bean sprouts and whose homemade chomchom can put Ganguram to shame.

A few years ago, in my novice party hosting days, in a moment of imaginary self-confidence, I invited a good number of people, more than could possibly fit into my one bedroom apartment. My kitchen was small, I barely had enough cooking utensils and I didn't even know half the people I had managed to invite. Fortunately, many of them declined the invitation, yet what remained was still a large contingent. I was young and rather foolish in the home department and had no clue about how I would serve dinner to this descending mass. My close friend R came to the rescue, lending me her heavy duty kadhai and suggesting that I outsource some of the dishes, especially the fish. 'Get the fish and mutton from Ganesh. It is impossible for you to make rui kaalia or kosha mangsho for all these people,' she professed wisely. 'But don't tell anyone it is from Ganesh. Tell them you made it at home.' Homemade was apparently in demand.

R had clearly underestimated the Bengali ladies. With their clever tongues, sharp eyes and years of experience, they could clearly see that the mutton I so confidently claimed as my own was actually sourced from a caterer. 'Doesn't this taste exactly like Ganesh's kosha mangsho? Are you sure you cooked this?' one of them asked, raising a shapely eyebrow. I was sweating buckets and managed to nod warily. 'Can you give me the recipe?' the lady continued, clearly having no intention of giving up. I froze. There was no recipe. Not in my possession, at least. I had yet to taste Ganesh's dish. Stuttering, I looked around when R came to my rescue. 'From the internet. Have you checked? There are very good recipes there. We will forward it to you.' Though she still looked a little doubtful, the lady's eyebrows settled down.

So when I say that at a weekend party rosogolla making, salad eating, svelte Bengali women are no less demanding than Hindi soap opera mothers-in-law, you have to believe me.

They look down upon a meal that lacks at least two vegetable dishes, a fish curry and something to do with mutton. It suffices to say that a meal planned without a Bengali chaatni as accompaniment can only be an act of rebellion or plain idiocy, making for years of hushed gossip around the block. Rapturous gushes of 'Oh, you have lost so much weight!' might help, but only under certain circumstances.

What's with Chutney Mary

Wiki says: 'Chutney (Hindi: चटनी) is a loan word incorporated into English from Hindi and describes a condiment used in ... South Asian cuisines. Chutneys usually contain an idiosyncratic but complementary spice and vegetable mix.'

Chutney is such a global favorite that many cities around the world have a restaurant called Chutney Mary.

It was a hot, sticky day in August, the kind that sends salty rivulets down your spine even in North America. A month ago, I had sent out invitations to forty adults and their twenty children for a Bengali meal at my place. It was my daughter's birthday and like all true-blue Bong mothers, I needed to celebrate it by feeding goat meat to forty-odd Bong adults. The children could just run around in the backyard and soak themselves in the sprinkler. I did not care. Birthdays are not about kids after all, at least not if you are a Bong kid. My real test lay in what the Bong community thought I had accomplished in the kitchen on the day.

I had hyperventilated for weeks over the menu. I had made excel sheets, statistically estimated in weight per human goat meat consumption and then extrapolated it to an exorbitant figure, which I then ordered from the halal meat store. A similar process was followed for fish and when MS Excel crashed under the pressure, it was unanimously decided that a shellfish would have to do what a sweet river fish could not.

I had been chopping bags of onions, making truck loads of ginger-garlic paste and swearing like a pro for two days before the party. As much as I like food and cooking, I have realized that a smaller audience suits me better. I am very happy cooking for my family of four or a group of fifteen friends, but just the logistics involved for sixty-odd people gives me the heebie-jeebies. 'Works well under pressure' will look perfect on my resumé, but I have been doing this for the last seven years and honestly, nothing good has come out of it.

Birthdays in my childhood were much simpler, really. I am a child of the 70s, and in my middle class Bengali family all a birthday translated to was paayesh, a new dress, touching feet of the elders and a crinkled ten-rupee note pushed into eager hands. A big pack of éclairs or Parle orange candies for school – this was the most exciting part. Cakes, balloons, candles and coloured paper streamers? Nah, those were completely unnecessary.

Instead, Ma would spend all morning in the kitchen, stirring paayesh, spreading soaked grains of rice on the newspaper to make a sweet yellow pulao, grating onion and ginger for doi maachh and pitting dates for tomato chutney. A couple of friends who lived nearby were asked to come and have dinner with a casual invitation of 'Aaj raatey kheye jash'. They came dressed in knee-length frocks, carrying thin books by Russian publishers, clumsily wrapped in solid coloured tissue paper. After a game of Ludo we sat down for a dinner of mishti pulao, fish curry, chutney and paayesh in scalloped silver bowls and, just like that, you were a year older.

Breaking my nostalgic reverie, the H-man said, 'That is how it should be.' From his prone position, a la Lord Vishnu on the couch, he philosophically muttered, 'One year just seamlessly merges into another on the day and nothing momentous like five pressure cookers full of rezala needs to be made or stressed over.'

But what does he know? It is not really about me or the birthday girl. There are higher things at stake, like the Bengali community and their expectations from me, the new Bong Mom on the block.

On the day of distress aka party, I was up early. I had had nightmares involving the caterer, to whom I had outsourced one hundred vegetable chops. In his squeaky voice, he had proclaimed that he could not make chops because there were no potatoes in the market. I woke up feeling nervous.

After clearing doubts about the caterer, I set to task, taking out trays and trays of cooked food from the refrigerator and putting them in the oven. Though I had been cooking all week, it had to look like the food had been cooked just that morning. By the time the party started, both me and the kitchen had to feign the stress-free spotless look, a difficult task to pull off at the best of times.

When I had taken out all the food trays and counted them three times, it was apparent that one was missing. I took every possible thing out of the refrigerator, from the half-eaten mould-grown gouda cheese to my pearl studded earring that had been missing for a year. Yet I could not find the elusive tray. There was no possible place I could have hidden it away for safekeeping.

It then dawned on me that between one tray of aloor dom, three of mutton rezala and two of prawn malaikari I had forgotten all about the chaatni. The tomato chaatni, for which I had got the choicest two pounds of fresh plump tomatoes on the vine from the farmer's market and mejdool dates from the Arabic market, had not been cooked. In ordinary circumstances I would have said 'Nahiiiiinnn' with my hands on the sides of my head while the dishwasher, oven and refrigerator revolved around in slow motion. Instead, I took a deep breath and set about chopping my tomatoes.

There was red gooey disaster all around and when my tomato chutney finally started its bubble on the stove top, the first guest rang the door bell. I wanted to clean it all up with a swish of Windex, but I let it be. This, after all, was the real scene.

TOMATO KHEJUR ER CHAATNI
Tomato and date chutney

Tomato chaatni was my staple diet as a kid. That and chhanar dalna. I don't remember eating much else as a five-year-old. My memory may have gone bad, but the red tomato chutney still glistens in the steel tiffin carrier that my mom, accompanied by the help, would bring for school lunch every day until second grade. To me tomato chaatni means a safe haven amidst strict nuns, new friends and a foreign language that I didn't understand.

I have made tomato chaatni pretty often and never felt that it lacked anything until we were at a party at my friend's place.

My friend is a really good cook and usually the quality and variety of the spread at her parties is unnerving. She is one of those domestic divas who can fry up seventy vegetable chops without a pleat budging from her sari. On this particular evening, amidst the rustling chiffons and the conscious Satya Pauls, all I noticed was the tomato chaatni.

Deep red in colour and studded with raisins, dates and aam shotto, it tasted heavenly. It was the piece which dazzled and was a perfect finale to a wonderful meal.

As I licked my fingers and savoured the chutney while others shoved empty plastic plates in the trash and talked about their daughters' upcoming recitals, I realized there was a tang in that chutney that was missing in mine. I shrugged it off and attributed it to her superior cooking skills.

Later, when I asked, she told me she had added some tamarind chutney to the tomato chaatni and that was the secret to its tangy taste. And then I remembered Ma adding a little tamarind pulp to her tomato chaatni too. How could I have forgotten? In fact, Ma would sometimes add a whole tamarind, pits and all, to the tomato chaatni. Now that I remember I can hear the clatter of the deep brown tamarind pits on the steel plate as I sucked them out clean.

More than just the tamarind pulp, the sweet-sour-spicy tamarind chutney really lends a nice dimension to the tomato chaatni and makes it delicious, so do try it next time. Khejur or dates is the perfect accompaniment for the tomatoes in the chutney and that is how it is usually made in a Bengali home. The aam shotto or aam papad/dried sweet mango slices is another delicious addition to the traditional Bengali tomato chaatni.

Good quality juicy tomatoes are the key ingredient here. So try to get vine-ripened tomatoes from your local haat or the farmers' market the day you plan to cook it.

5 juicy plump tomatoes
20 chopped pitted dates
¼ cup golden raisins
1 tsp ginger juice (grate ginger and squeeze to get the juice)
2 tbsp tamarind chutney (optional but lends a nice taste)

Spices for tempering
2 tsp black mustard seeds
2 dry red chilli

½ cup sugar
¼ tsp turmeric powder
¼ tsp salt
1 tbsp mustard oil

Spices for bhaja masala
1 tsp cumin and 1 red chilli dry roasted and ground to a powder

♪ Wash and chop the red tomatoes in large-ish chunks. Each tomato should be chopped in 8–10 pieces. Chop pitted dates in halves or in thin slices.

♪ Heat oil in a deep-bottomed sauce pan.

♪ Temper the hot oil with black mustard seeds and dry red chilli. Cover with a lid to avoid having the mustard dance a salsa around your kitchen.

Note: you can avoid the chilli if you don't want the dish too spicy.

♪ When the mustard sputters, add the chopped tomatoes, a pinch of turmeric, a little salt and sauté them. Then cover and cook the tomatoes at low heat. The juicy tomatoes will release a lot of liquid and will cook in their own juice. Every minute or so, remove the lid and stir well.

♪ When the tomatoes are nearly done, add the chopped dates, golden raisins and stir well. If you have aam shotto, add some chopped now. Add the ginger juice. Add about ¼–½ cup water and cook for a few more minutes till the tomatoes have totally disintegrated and thoroughly cooked to a soft pulp.

♪ Add sugar, mix well, adjust for salt and sugar and then let the chutney simmer and reduce to a thick consistency.

♪ Here is a small tip. To make the chutney tangy, add 2 tbsp tamarind chutney to it. You can use a store-bought one or make one of your own using tamarind pulp. This really gives the chutney a sweet-tangy taste instead of just sweet.

♪ Before serving, sprinkle with dry roasted cumin and red chilli powder, the bhaja masala. Serve to accompany a meal. You can also use it as a dip.

The Chutney Tales

The chutney in a Bengali household is almost always prepared fresh and is eaten as a course of a lunch or a dinner to accent the meal. Different regions in India specialize in the ingredients used for their chutneys and Bengal specializes in chutney made with fruits like raw mango, tomato, pineapple and papaya and even with fish, especially the head of hilsa.

Traditionally, the Bengali meal ends with a dessert, and the chaatni, a sweet and sour preparation, precedes it. In a Bengali wedding feast, when the server tosses out crisp papad and ladles plastic pineapple chutney carelessly onto your plate, you know the meal is about to end. But for me, chaatni is an accompaniment to the meal rather than the finale. Instead of relegating it to a position at the end of the meal, I almost always start with it. When I dip my fingers in the chaatni bowl and lick them off, I know the meal laid out in front of me is going to be special.

AAM-ANAROSHER CHAATNI
Mango pineapple chutney

My favourite chaatni, after tomato, are those made with mangoes — aamer ambol and aamer chaatni. These days I like the latter more than the former. I like the soupy kind of aamer ambol flecked with black kalonji on hot summer days. I can drink it by the bowlful. On other days I make the thicker aam chaatni that looks like clusters of bright sunshine laid out on the table. Here I have added pineapple to mangoes for a sweet–sour effect. You can skip the pineapple and just use mangoes to make the mango chutney.

1 raw green mango, roughly peeled and then chopped in cubes	Salt to taste
	½ tsp turmeric powder
1 cup pineapple chunks from a can or fresh (optional)	2 tsp oil (vegetable or mustard)
Spices for tempering	½ tsp paanch-phoron dry roasted and ground to a powder along with a roasted dry red chilli
1 tsp mustard seeds	
1 dry red chilli	
2/3 cup sugar. A little more might be needed if the mango is very sour.	

- Wash and roughly peel 1 raw green mango. You don't have to peel it very smoothly and can leave the peel on in strips. Chop the mango into small pieces (cubes). If using fresh pineapple, chop pineapple in pieces smaller than the mango.

- Heat the oil in a kadhai/frying pan. Add the mustard seeds and dry red chilli. The mustard seeds will sputter and dance with a war cry, so take precaution.

- As soon as the mustard seeds start hissing, add the chopped mangoes. Add a pinch of turmeric powder and sauté the mangoes. Next, add the pineapple. Sprinkle salt. Sauté till the mangoes and pineapple turn a nice yellow because of the turmeric and soften a little.

- Add salt to taste and about 1 cup water. There should be enough water to cook the mangoes and pineapple both, so adjust the level accordingly. The chaatni should be on the thicker side, so add water moderately. Mix and cover and cook till both mangoes and pineapple are almost done. Check with the spatula to see if they have softened. Fresh pineapple will take longer to cook.

♪ Add sugar and mix well. If the pineapple is sweet, the sugar mentioned in the ingredients list should be enough. However, Bengali chutneys are usually sweeter than the average, so a little more sugar could be added if desired. If the water has dried up at this point, add a little more water. Cook and reduce the water till you get a thick consistency and the mangoes and pineapples are soft but not mashed up.

♪ Dry roast paanch-phoron and one dry red chilli till you get a nice aroma, then cool and dry grind it. Sprinkle this powder on the chaatni and it's ready to serve!

Jain Auntie's Tamarind Date Chutney

If you have noticed, the West is as obsessed with chutneys as it is with bejewelled elephants. I honestly did not know about the chutney obsession until I saw Patak's (a popular UK brand) bottled sweet tamarind chutney in the aisles of Stop & Shop, our neighbourhood grocery store.

I was then new to this country. The first froth of excitement had fizzled out and I was at the nostalgic stage, missing home. Days had fallen into a routine. 'How I miss Doordarshan' ... mope, mope, mope... 'I so miss prolonged power cuts' ... more moping. The only thing I looked forward to each evening was the visit to the grocery store. Until then I had been used to the kirana stores in India, my favourite being the small store owned by Maulbi Saab. He sold lavender Chelpark inks, fresh white bread, 2B yellow pencils with pointed tips and there was a long, deep wooden counter with grooves running along the shop's length separating Maulbi Saab, the master, from the humble customer. Every time I went there, I had to make a strong decision, justify my purchase, and then gather enough courage to say it loud enough to reach his ears on the other side. Buying personal hygiene stuff was plain appalling!

Coming from a kirana store upbringing, the American grocery stores held me enthralled. Their precisely spaced aisles, their cold freezer doors, their perfect porcelain-like red gala apples balanced in a pyramid and their trust that allowed me to touch, feel and smell every item on their shelves had me in raptures. I spent a lot of those first, hot summer days in the coolness of what most would label monotonous interiors. Only, I did not find it monotonous. At every turn a Glade green apple candle, a Pledge wipe, a frozen bag of bagel bites that cooked themselves in the microwave, surprised me. I caressed them, running my hand along the smooth exterior of a curvy bottle of olive oil; I smelled the seas when I took a sprinkle of oregano in my cupped palms and dove my nose in it. I had enough time to idle around those aisles discovering things I did not know or need and it was my first time seeing chutney in glamorous bottles, jostling for space with Tabasco sauce.

Till then, chutney was what Ma made at home or the bhajiawala doled out with the samosas and kachoris at the corner store. Coconut chutney was something that was always, always served out of shiny steel containers along with petal-soft white idlis by the dosa cart vendor who came by Tuesday evenings, announcing his presence with the signature beat of his metallic spatula along the iron griddle. However much you liked that coconut chutney, you could never buy it in a bottle anywhere. And the green and red chutney that the vada-pav seller slathered on his pav? I could give anything for a bottle of that, but did he sell the chutney alone? No, never. Pickles and sauces in bottles I could understand, but chutney?

That Patak chutney bottle with the purple lid kindled in me a strange kinship towards the store and the country I had immigrated to. I obligingly forgave the lady at the check-out counter who said 'I love India. Where is it? By Iraq?' How could a country that loved chutney enough to pile its shelves with it be alien to me? This is what I told myself.

Eventually, I realized that Patak's chutney would not do for me what my Ma's chaatni could. But that was much later. For a long time, I subscribed to Patak's date tamarind chutney with a fervour that I reserve for my daily *Times of India* horoscope. The tamarind chutney reminded me of our onetime neighbour, Jain Auntie, with her big round maroon bindi and tinkling glass bangles. She made the most amazing pickles and papads I have ever eaten. During winter, her backyard would be chock-a-block with glass jars of different shapes and sizes, each containing something submerged in layers of oil and spices in hues of red, brown and yellow. There were fat red chillies stuffed with fennel and coriander, sunning in their oil bath. White cauliflower florets, orange carrot slices, white radish. Name a vegetable, and she would serve it to you, pickled.

Inspired by her, Ma made a variety of homemade pickles, papad and potato chips for a couple of winters. Those were delicious and busy winters. Potatoes sliced wafer-thin were set out to dry in the sun on stretched-out cotton sarees. Spiced tapioca papad, rice papad and lentil papad gave them company. I had little to do except to keep watch at high noon when Ma took her nap and the crows on the mango tree cawed for attention. The raw, dry papads tasted as good as the fried ones and I often ate them if Ma wasn't looking.

Jain Auntie also cooked a very good dish of chhole. But she made it very rarely, twice a year to be precise, on her kids' birthdays. Her chhole was liberally doused with a tamarind chutney which I actually liked more than the main dish. Tired of hearing my laments about that tamarind chutney and chhole, Ma started making it at home, only she made ghugni instead of chhole. That did not bother me; it was the sour-sweet tamarind chutney I was after.

Ma would get a block of dried ripe tamarind, still moist and reddish brown in colour, wrapped up in a newspaper on the day of the chutney making. She would soak it in warm water and then rub the seeds off with her hands to take out the 'kaath'. The whole thing was then strained to get the pulp out. Ma would then boil the liquid and temper it with dry roasted cumin powder, salt and red chilli powder and sweeten it with jaggery. It was sweet, tangy and spicy, all at the same time.

This tamarind chutney, which looked like a brownish version of tar, was the best thing you could use to liven up a ghugni or to serve as a dip with aloor chop for tiffin or snacks. Once my mother got the hang of it, she would make it often and store it in glass jars for a week or two. It served many neighbourhood aunties who would drop in unannounced for a cup of tea in the afternoon and then continue their gossip over homemade papad with the chutney forming a tantalizing dip.

That was a different place, a different time. Tea was an integral part of the Bengali life and tea-time a sumptuous affair. Most people I encounter here do not drink tea. Even if they do, it is the weird stuff, the Echinacea tea, the dandelion tea, 'please-don't-drink-me' tea. Only rarely, if ever, do they make the simmering-on-the-stove, frothy, milky, sweet, dhaba-style Indian tea and serve it with a myriad of snacks.

TETUL KHEJURER CHUTNEY
Tamarind date chutney

¾ cup pitted dates, chopped	1 tsp bhaja masala
¼ cup seedless tamarind	Salt to taste
½ cup brown sugar	Add a few drops of mustard
½ tsp red chilli powder	oil at the end if you wish

♪ Bring 3 cups water to boil.

♪ Add the dates and tamarind to it. Simmer for about 20 minutes. When the dates have softened, add the sugar, red chilli powder, bhaja masala and salt.

♪ Now let it simmer for 8–10 more minutes. By this time the dates will have turned into mush.

♪ Cool the mixture and puree in a blender. Strain to remove any fibre. You can skip the straining if you like bits and pieces of fruit in your chutney like I do.

♪ Add a few drops of mustard oil for the final kick. Refrigerate and use within a month. You can thin this chutney and drizzle it on chaat. The thicker version can be used as a dip for anything that is deep-fried.

DHONEPATA CHUTNEY
Coriander chutney

This is a no-cook, fresh and vibrant chutney that my mom makes. During summer she uses green mango and adds mint leaves. The chutney has 'fresh' written all over it and should be made to say so. I use it as a dip for corn chips when not using it as a chutney for deep-fried goodies.

½ cup coriander leaves, chopped	Quarter of a lime's worth of juice
4 green chillies	Salt to taste
2 cloves garlic	½ tsp sugar
1" piece peeled ginger	Few drops of mustard oil

♪ Put everything in the blender except salt and sugar. Make a fine paste with a splash of water, a tsp or so. Add a little more lime juice if needed. Add salt to taste and sugar. Adjust to taste. Mix well. Use as a dip for starters.

The Bhaja Masala Tales

Bhaja masala, the brown, sharp spice powder that every Bengali kitchen stores in a small jar, is like fairy dust. You use it cautiously, in small amounts, aware of the changes it can make to your food. Not an everyday spice like cumin or coriander, it is to be sprinkled in small quantities on a ghugni, a pineapple chutney or put in an aloor chop. The secret recipe of bhaja masala is unique to every Bengali home and it seems presumptuous to put it in the framework of teaspoons and tablespoons.

A simple recipe of bhaja masala has just two ingredients: whole cumin and dry red chilli. Roast about ½ tsp cumin seeds till you get a nice roasted smell. Char the dry red chilli by holding directly on fire. Be careful with this step and don't burn the red chilli. Now grind both together to make a fine powder.

The second recipe has more going on. To make this, dry roast 1 tbsp each of cumin seeds, coriander seeds, fennel seeds, 6–7 cloves, 6–7 cardamom, 2 bay leaves, an inch and half of cinnamon stick and peppercorns according to your desired hotness level. Then just dry grind it to a powder. Store in an airtight jar for later use.

A few years ago, around the time of my birthday, I had expressed a wish for a relaxed evening and some time to myself. All I had in mind was a quiet evening at home where I could put my feet up, relax, drink my tea in peace and watch Food Network.

Instead, the H-man gave me a polka-dotted gift bag stuffed with coloured paper tissues. When I shoved my hand down below the confetti and pretty baubles, I found the exact thing which I had feared. A gift-card to a spa. A spa! What was the guy thinking?

If you must know, I am not the kind of woman who embraces spas with open arms. Neither is he. In fact, he was attracted by my well-oiled whiskers in the first place.

'Why would you want me to go to a spa?' I wailed. 'What would I do there? What would the spa people do with me? They would not even know where to start! And if

I stripped and lay down on their massage tables that would be the end of it.'

'You can get a haircut,' he suggested. It was clear he had his basics messed up. He did not know a spa from a salon and could be of no further help.

I was pretty depressed about this spa thing and, I have to admit, nervous too. Finally, I gathered the courage, took half a day off and went away to relax for two hundred dollars. The spa had a Middle Eastern theme going on and it was all dimmed lights and heavy satin curtains.

After a gruelling thirty minute sign-in session of S-for-Siberia, A-for-Alaska and N-for-Nantucket at the reception, I was given a four page questionnaire and asked to take a seat. I hadn't attempted a multiple choice questionnaire since my GRE. Not even the one in Femina which asks 'What would you do if you had bad breath and your fiancé were about to propose?' Compared to that, this one was really tough. The questions asked after my skin type and the kind of fragrance that soothes me. They asked after the location of my karmic centre, my sun sign and whether I had one partner or multiple. I did not have the whole day to waste and so just picked 'D' for every third question and 'B' for the others.

Fifteen minutes later, a young girl dressed like a gypsy with flowing sequined skirts, pierced belly and aquamarine eye-shadow took me in. She was clearly a school dropout who had as much an idea of gypsies as I did about micro-dermabrasion.

'Would you like something to drink?' the girl asked.

I asked for tea, hoping for a masala chai in keeping with the theme. Instead, she got me a sweet smelling pale liquid and called it lavender tea. 'It will help you relax, calm you and soothe your nerves,' she drawled, and wafted away.

The tea actually tasted like scented, tepid tap water. I took fast gulps. Piped Bedouin music floated through the room. I was slowly warming up to the whole spa idea and even trying to relax when the girl floated in again.

'Whaddya wanna have?' she asked. 'Errm, nothing. I am actually good,' I said. 'Organic Peeling, Kerala Coconut Massage, Sea Salt Glow, Shiatsu,' she chanted like the waitress at a Chinese restaurant.

I wanted to go home. This was beyond my universe of knowledge.

Fifteen minutes later I found myself stripped and dressed in nothing but a robe in a dimly lit room. I was being rubbed with hot stones in rhythmic strokes. 'Euphoria massage,' the gypsy girl said. The room smelled of cinnamon, orange and ginger, like a warm bread pudding. I groaned and made orgasmic sounds and then I passed out. I probably snored.

When I woke up hours later there was a card by the table.

'The facility is now closed. See you tomorrow morning. If you wake up and happen to be hungry, there is some lavender tea in the lounge,' it read.

How I got myself out of there at 9 p.m. is another story. Back home, all I wanted was a steaming cup of masala chai. I needed to relax.

Every Bong Girl Needs Her Tiffin

And a cup of hot tea to go with it.

Over the years, my love for tea has grown to four cups a day of sweetened Red Label with a touch of milk. A strongly brewed tea is the light at the end of the tunnel, sorry, the highway I take home.

My drive back from work through insane traffic is crappy and takes just under an hour on the best days. It is fraught with nail-biting drama, drivers who apply mascara while steering the wheel and Minis that have sprouted wings. If a detour or road block is thrown into this mix, I am just short of passing out. When I finally reach home, unscathed, in one piece, all I want is to be welcomed with a cup of steaming hot tea. I would give anything, even my fear of consuming gallons of oil, for a plateful of hot-off-the-kadhai peyaji on the side.

But do I get that? No.

Instead, every evening, I measure out cups of water and milk and set them to boil. While the girls chatter non-stop, I watch the water, waiting for it to come to a rolling boil. The three year old clambers up my knees and says 'Mamma, I want to be a baker when I am big.' 'Good idea sweetie, you can make us yum cakes,' I say, patiently waiting for the milk and water to simmer and froth. She says 'No mamma, not that kind. I want to be to be the Bengali "bekaar". The one who does nothing'. Sighing I put in a teaspoon of Lipton Red Label, sweeten my tea with sugar and then dunk my Marie biscuit in before I take a sip. The kids get a Marie biscuit each and they are allowed to dunk their biscuits in my steaming cup. Their baby hands falter and often a sliver of Marie sinks into my tea, its lumpy form settling at the bottom of my cup. Some days I don't mind. On rough days I do; I just want to sip my tea in peace without a lump of biscuit in the dregs.

Marie or a pack of Parle G is the extent of my indulgence on weekdays. That way, I'm a shame to Bongs. Bongs treat their evening snack or jolkhabar with far more sincerity than this.

For a Bengali, jolkhabar or tiffin is as important a meal as breakfast, lunch and dinner. They revel in their 'cha er sathe ta' culture, a take-off on the British high tea, where light sandwiches and pastries are replaced by liberal helpings of mustard oil. Depending on the gravity of the occasion, it can range from simplistic to an elaborate samosa-fish fry-luchi affair. At the most basic level of snack is muri-chanachur – puffed rice mixed with spicy chanachur – a homebody cousin of the sassy jhaalmuri.

Jhaalmuri is a phenomenon I was first introduced to on a train journey. Puffed rice, in small packets made of yellowed newspaper, was handed to me through the iron grills of the train window. A sickle-shaped sliver of coconut was balanced on top. Beneath it was the muri flecked with tiny pieces of purple onion, green chilli and brown roasted peanuts, suspended around the smell of pungent mustard oil. I was hooked. Does it get better than this? For that you need to tip the packet into your cupped hand and take a mouthful. The flavours rush into each other, and you experience bliss. You look at the mundane packet of week-old newspaper with new respect and life is never the same again.

Though I have found jhaalmuri at street corners, bus-stations, movie theatres, fair grounds and almost everywhere a Bong can go, for me it personifies a journey, travel, the call of the road. Even now on my visits to India, I take a train or bus to my in-laws' house just so I can instruct the jhaalmuri man with the tin box and multiple steel containers: 'Dada, jhaal beshi, tel ta olpo.'

I am deep in my jhaalmuri reverie when I am sharply nudged in the ribs by my older child.

'Mommy, tomorrow is International Day at school. You need to send a snack,' she says, thrusting a flyer in my face.

'What snack? And why didn't you tell me earlier?'

Send in any kid-friendly snack from your culture for twenty kids and two teachers, the flyer reads.

'I did tell you last week, you said okay,' the precocious kid continues.

That might be true. My survival tactic is to say 'okay' to any question that pertains to the future.

'Mommy, can I colour my hair purple when I am twenty?'

'Okay.'

'Mommy, can I watch TV all day when I am grown up?'

'Okay.'

'Mommy, can you send snacks for International Day next week?'

'Okay.'

And now I am in big trouble.

I try to think fast. Samosas? Perfect for kids. I call the friendly neighbourhood Bengali caterer who has saved me on many such occasions. 'I want to order twenty-five samosas. Make them non-spicy, ekdom jhaal noy. Also no nuts,' I say authoritatively with the confidence of a woman who orders a variety of samosas every evening.

Mrs Caterer is clearly PMSing. 'Hobe na!' she declares. 'Without peanuts and chillies? It's impossible. Make it yourself this time.' My jaws open wide. Did she just ask me to make my own samosas?

She has a point. If she can make 25 samosas at a moment's notice, why can't I? It's my kid after all. And it is my kid's darn school that had this brilliant idea of International Day.

But clearly I am no Super Mom to whip up 25 samosas on a winter evening. I think hard. What other snacks belong to my culture? All I can think of is hot, spicy aloor chop served with crisp muri and mustard oil or vegetable chop stuffed with sweet beets and carrots. Crispy pakoras fried in gallons of hot oil, golden brown and crunchy. Even a plateful of yellow ghugni liberally sprinkled with onions and coriander. These are the snacks my mother served along with steaming cups of Darjeeling tea in the evenings. She made them effortlessly, with an ease I cannot even pretend to have.

But I am not too sure about these kids. Was it okay to put finely chopped raw red onion in food served to 20 Caucasian kids? What if their parents sue me because the green chilli was too hot or the mustard oil caused them to sneeze?

Why do we eat such difficult snacks? Why aren't chicken nuggets the national snack of India?

'What about Haldiram's bhujia?' my daughter helpfully suggests. For a brief moment I want to hug her and stuff two of those packets from my pantry into her school bag. But better sense prevails. I have an image to live up to and sending a packet of bhujia for International Day does not fit it. 'Responsible, concerned about healthy eating, loves to cook for the kids' are some of the things I like to say about myself on my blog. Didn't I say I lack foresight?

Finally, I decide on maachher chop. These fish croquettes are healthy, brimming with Omega 3, relatively easy to make and eminently suitable for a bunch of seven- and eight-year-olds. I get to work quickly. The tilapia filet is brought out from the freezer to be thawed. The potatoes are put to boil. The warm kitchen hums with activity.

Chop, chop, grate, grind. The family gets to work. I omit the green chilli and any semblance of spice, for the sake of little kids and only add a dash of garam masala. The H-man rolls up his sleeves and fashions oblong croquettes out of the mix. Tomorrow morning they will be rolled in bread crumbs and shallow-fried. The kids at school are going to love it.

MAACHHER CHOP
Spicy fish croquettes
(makes about 14 chops)

2 tilapia/cod/bhetki fillet	20 golden raisins
1 cup mashed potatoes	½ tsp sugar
1 cup chopped red onion	½ tsp salt. Add more to taste.
1 clove garlic, minced	Rock salt for sprinkling
1 tsp garlic paste	2 tsp oil for making the
1 tsp ginger paste	stuffing and ½ cup for frying
4 green chillies, chopped fine	the croquette.
1 tsp lime juice	Fresh or store-bought
1 tsp garam masala powder	breadcrumbs seasoned with
½ tsp red chilli powder	salt and pepper.
1 tsp coriander chutney (in	Egg wash made by beating
the absence of this, use	1 egg and 1 tbsp water.
freshly chopped coriander)	

ꝃ   Cook the fish in the microwave for 5–6 minutes. Time may vary so
     I suggest you do it in intervals of 3 minutes. Crumble the cooked
     fish to give you a little more than 1 cup cooked fish. Cook 1 large
     potato and mash it to yield 1 cup mashed potatoes. Put the
     cooked fish and mashed potato in a big mixing bowl. Add 1 tsp
     lime juice. Mix the fish and potatoes with your hand to make a
     smooth mix.

ꝃ   Heat about 2 tsp oil in a frying pan. Add minced garlic. When you
     get the fragrance, add onion and fry until soft and brown at the
     edges. Add garlic paste, ginger paste and green chillies chopped
     fine. Fry for a couple more minutes.

ꝃ   Add this to the fish and potato mix. Next add fresh garam masala,
     red chilli powder, coriander chutney (or fresh chopped coriander),
     salt to taste, golden raisins and a little sugar. Taste at this point
     and adjust the seasonings. Mix everything well with your hand till
     you get a smooth, dough-like mix. Fashion your chop either in flat
     discs or make oblong shapes.

ꝃ   Now prepare for frying and set up the following cycle:
     Egg wash → A flat platter with seasoned bread crumbs → Hot oil
     for shallow frying.

ꝃ   Dip the chop/croquette in egg wash → roll in bread crumbs →
     shallow fry till golden brown on both sides.

     *Note: After rolling in bread crumbs, I usually leave the chops in the
     refrigerator for an hour or two. Then I lightly roll them in bread crumbs
     for the second time and then shallow-fry.*

ꝃ   Sprinkle with rock salt or chaat masala. Serve with chopped
     onion, mustard and ketchup.

BEGUNI
Spicy eggplant fritters

Every year in Boishakh, the first month of the Bengali New Year, the Kal-Boishakhi or nor'westers arrive, heralding the fierce rain storms that sweep through the plains of Bengal. It is unlike any rain I have ever seen; urgent and strong, fiercely pushing aside leaves, twigs, the fine brown dust and all that is old as it marches on its way. In its wake remain broken tree limbs, fallen wires and flooded lanes.

If it were mid-April, the ominous dark clouds gathering in the sky and a wind rustling up were signal enough for us to prepare for a storm. 'The clothes will get wet!' my mother would panic and we would run up to the terrace. As the wind picked up and the window shutters banged fiercely, we rushed downstairs, trying to close all the windows as we went. And then the rains came, arriving in all their grandeur, the fat round pellets going pitter-patter until we were consumed by the rain sound.

Rainy days were earmarked for khichuri. And of course there was beguni to go with it. A plump, purple eggplant would be sliced into rounds of just the right thickness and soaked in salted water. Meanwhile, Ma poured besan into a bowl. She sprinkled salt over it and threw in a few jet-black seeds of kalonji, half a teaspoon of red chilli powder, a pinch of baking powder and slowly added water to make a smooth batter. Then the kadhai was placed on the stove. The sharp smell of heating mustard oil slowly filled the crevices of our home. The hot oil hissed as the batter-coated eggplant slices touched it and then there was the familiar sound of 'chyank–chok', the chatter of deep frying. Hot, brown, crispy begunis were piled up on the kitchen counter. With a sprinkle of rock salt, they were ready to be devoured.

Eggplant chopped in thin rounds or semi circles. Depending on the kind of eggplant you are using, chop about 10 rounds and semicircles.

For batter
1   cup chickpea flour
¾   cup water

¼   tsp baking powder
½   tsp red chilli powder
1   tbsp rice flour
¼   tsp nigella seeds
    Salt to taste
    Chaat masala or rock salt for sprinkling on the fritters (optional)
    Oil for deep frying

🍃 Wash the eggplant well, pat dry. Then slice vertically in thin rounds or semicircles of 1/4 inch thickness. For a plump eggplant, half-moon or semicircle is preferred. Smear with salt and keep aside for 10–15 mins

🍃 Make a batter of the chickpea flour with all the ingredients listed under 'batter'. Add water gradually to make a batter as thick as pakoda batter.

🍃 Heat oil for deep frying in a kadhai. Dip the eggplant slices in the chickpea flour batter so that they are uniformly coated and then gently slide into the hot oil. Fry till golden brown on both sides. Remove with a slotted spoon and drain on a paper towel.

🍃 Sprinkle some chaat masala or pink salt on the beguni for that additional zing.

Food by the High Road aka Aloor Chop

My mother, queen of umpteen delicious dishes, abhors street food. Despite her healthy disrespect for street food, I have a reverence for it quite similar to the way I felt about Mills & Boons in high school. Forbidden but tempting.

Ma, having grown up in the moffusils of Bengal, had an almost uncanny fear of Kolkata street food. She thought anything cooked and served on the street could only bring cholera, jaundice and disaster. You can well imagine how this phobia of hers had a serious impact on my upbringing. My school days were spent longingly watching the aloo-tikki and chhole-chaatwala serving a myriad schoolgirls his delicious-looking fare on badly washed steel plates. All I was allowed to buy, once a month, was a packet of spicy potato chips or a bar of golden ice cream from the cart. It was torture.

It was her good fortune that we did not live in Kolkata or its suburbs where it was easier to find phuchka, deep fried telebhaja and aloor chop than a taxi to take you to Kalighat.

But on our annual visits to my grandmother's house in north Calcutta, things would change radically. Ma would be too busy shopping and movie-watching to bother about the bacterial content in telebhaja and every afternoon I would plead with my Mama or Ma's cousins to buy me aloor chop and chingrir chop. Some days they would comply, as even they needed an excuse to feast on muri-telebhaja in the evening.

In the narrow bylanes of Dida's house was a little telebhaja shop popular in the locality as 'Buri'r Dokan' – the old woman's shop, and it was her deep-fried goodies that enticed us. It was a narrow sliver of a shop tucked between a shiny sweet store named 'Kalika Mishtanno Bhandar' and a small ladies tailoring facility. The shop's once-saffron walls were blackened with soot from the pump stove and a naked 60-watt bulb hung from a stray wire on the ceiling, dim with its efforts to shed light on the affairs going on beneath. By the stove sat Buri, a thin wiry frame wrapped in a narrow bordered sari, white hair pulled in a tiny knot. With one hand she swirled the besan batter, dipped an eggplant or discs of spiced mashed potatoes in it and then let them fall with assurance into the sea of hot oil that bubbled in a big blackened kadhai. At the same time, her other hand held a big slotted spoon that turned the fritters over, shook out the excess oil and dumped them into an equally blackened wicker basket.

Her son and her grandson were her helpers, shaping the fritters, taking orders from the throng of hungry people who crowded around and serving them in oil-stained newspaper packets. Lorai'er chop, chingrir chop, mochar chop, aloor chop – these were the names scrawled in Bengali on the black chalkboard that hung by the side of the store. The shop smelled of desire and deep-frying.

To me that shop was a symbol of feminine power and it has long been my secret dream to open a chai shop on the lower level of Grand Central, where I shall sell hot fried pakoras on rainy days.

ALOOR CHOP
Spiced potato fritters

Aloor chop is the most primitive Bengali fast food, and came long before the advent of the ubiquitous egg roll and chowmein stalls. Every neighbourhood in Calcutta sells it. It is a bit difficult to emulate the taste of the roadside aloor chop at home because you lack basic ingredients like dust, grime and the blackened oil that every popular shop swears by. But then that's what makes Indian street food so unique and tasty.

Makes about 14–16 fritters

For the chop

5 medium potatoes

1 medium onion, chopped fine

3 fat garlic cloves minced

1 tbsp minced ginger

4–5 green chilli chopped fine (adjust to taste)

2 tbsp chopped coriander leaves (optional)

1 tsp cumin powder

Red chilli powder to taste

Salt to taste

2 tsp mustard oil

For the batter

1 cup chickpea flour

1 tbsp rice flour

¼ tsp baking powder

Salt to taste

¾ cup water

For frying:

½ cup oil (mustard oil is preferred)

- Boil the potatoes, peel the skin and mash. Use your fingers or a masher.

- Heat 2 tsp oil in a kadhai. Add the finely chopped garlic, minced ginger, the green chillies and the onion. Sauté till the onion wilts and is pinkish brown. Add the cumin powder and red chilli powder and sauté for a minute.

- Add the mashed potatoes. Add salt, coriander leaves and mix the masala well with the potatoes. Remove from heat. Add a few drops of mustard oil to the potatoes if you want. Taste and adjust for seasoning.

♪ Make small balls of the mashed potatoes which are now spiced with the masala. Flatten them between your palms and place them on a lightly greased surface. They should be really flat and not thick like aloo tikki.

♪ Mix all the ingredients for the batter together, adding water gradually. The batter should be tight as it has to form a coating on the chop. Dip the chop in the batter and coat it uniformly.

♪ Deep fry in hot oil. Keep heat at medium and fry to golden brown. Remove with a slotted spoon/strainer and drain excess oil by placing the fried chop on a kitchen towel. Sprinkle some chaat masala or rock salt on the chop before serving.

The Story of the Egg Roll

It was one of those late Friday nights. We had just finished dinner. Copious amounts of aloo posto and musurir dal had been consumed. The kids had been put to bed. The H-man and I were squabbling over whether to watch a movie (I had selected a chocolate-dipped chick-flick) or just continue watching what Neanderthals had had for dinner on National Geographic. Neanderthals won. I was grouchy. Ma chose this as the best time to call, only to say:

'Baby mashi's sister Dolly is coming to the USA.'

'Yeah, okay, so?' I was clueless as to why this was relevant to my life.

'Arre, I mean she is going to New York, her son is there now. You should go and meet her.' My mother's voice was rich and energetic with morning tea and cream crackers.

'But I don't even know her, Ma.'

'Of course you do. Remember she came to your wedding

a day early. She is your Baba's third cousin's aunt. We are family.' My mother thinks everyone is family, including the mailman.

'Oh, is she the one who gifted us that ugly tea set which you then recycled at our neighbour's daughter's wedding?'

Ma ignored the tea set reference and said, 'You must go see them. She lands at JFK tomorrow.'

'I am not going to see some distant aunt of Baba's. I barely know her!'

'No, no but you must. Durga Pujo starts next Friday. You have to meet Dolly over the weekend.'

'Okay, Ma, what is it? What have you done? Have you sent something again?' My mother has this habit of sending gifts for the family through anyone coming to the US. If possible she would be standing at Dum Dum Airport handing out plastic bags from Pantaloons or Shoppers Stop to all and sundry. Once we had to travel three hours across states to collect a packet of nolen gur that Ma had sent.

'Well, it is Pujo, how could I not send something for my granddaughters? You go and get it from Dolly mashi tomorrow. New York is only next door. I don't know why you grumble so much.'

With that she ended the conversation. My goal for Saturday had been carved in stone. I was going to New York City.

The next day, I found myself in one of the quietest and most beautiful streets of New York. Climbing up the steps of a house with tall bay windows and a baroque facade, I was mighty impressed.

Dolly mashi's daughter-in-law opened the door for

me. Clad in Prada khakis and an Anne Klein cashmere, she desperately tried to look as Upper East as she could. With her shanka-pola and half a dozen gold bangles, the look whimpered and staggered to something like Aruna Irani meets Prada. Her faux accent didn't help either. Dolly mashi hugged me and complained about her arthritic knee. After an hour of small talk, plain water no ice, more small talk and neatly wrapped packets from my mother, I was let loose on the streets. Clearly Dolly mashi's daughter-in-law did not believe in food. My tummy was growling.

I trundled past Central Park, walking towards Times Square, now ravenous. New York is like Kolkata when it comes to street food. Sure, the phuchka is replaced by hot dogs and pretzels and caramel corn. But it is all there, warm smells emanating from every street corner. Given the clean surroundings, it doesn't taste half as good as the aloo kabli in Kolkata, but it will do. There are strapping young men in Greek carts selling gyros, perfect shavings of roasted shawarma meat wrapped with crunchy lettuce, onions and tomatoes in pita bread. The Bangladeshi carts selling biryani in Styrofoam boxes had a bevy of customers. But I walked past all this, for I had a destination in mind.

A few blocks shy of Times Square, between Fifth and Sixth Avenues, lies the Kati Roll Company. Their rolls are almost as good as the egg rolls in Kolkata. Soft paratha with a layer of egg wrapped around onions and tomatoes. They remind me of Hot Kati, the store at the corner of Park Street.

It is not every day that we can come all the way to New York City. But it is almost every day that the heart seeks an egg roll. The solution: you make your own, of course.

The H-man makes delicious egg rolls. Not only me, but everyone else who has had them vouches for his mastery. They are very close to the ones you can buy in Park Street, and his version is the quickest and easiest to make. He uses Malaysian Kawan paratha as the base and serves up a delicious roll in less than six minutes.

If you want the real deal I suggest you get out of your pyjamas and walk out to the nearest roll corner. Everyone else, get a pack of frozen paratha and proceed.

KOLKATA STYLE EGG ROLL

1 paratha for each roll. You can make your own paratha or buy the frozen ones.	**For garnish and stuffing:** Thinly sliced onion
1 egg for each roll	Finely chopped green chilli
1 tbsp whole milk	Lime juice
Salt to taste	Maggi Hot & Sweet ketchup
1–2 tsp vegetable oil for each roll	

♪ Buy good quality soft parathas, frozen or fresh. The quality of the paratha plays an important part in the egg roll. If you are making your own paratha, make the dough with maida and enough shortening that the paratha remains very soft and pliable. You can use tortilla, roti or the regular paratha, but it will not taste the same.

♪ Heat a tawa. Put the paratha on it and cook both sides. Remove and keep aside.

♪ In a separate bowl beat one egg with 1 tbsp whole milk and a little salt.

♪ Smear the tawa with oil and pour the egg mixture on it. Spread it out in a circle. Once the egg is a little cooked at the edges, put the paratha on top. When the edges of the egg start browning, flip the paratha together with the egg. Give it a couple of seconds.

♪ Remove and assemble the filling. The filling goes only on the egg side. The standard filling for a Kolkata egg roll is thinly sliced red onions, thinly chopped green chillies and thinly sliced cucumber. Squirt a little lime juice on them and put the filling in the centre. Add tomato ketchup in a thin squiggly line along the centre. Roll, wrap it up in foil or paper and eat.

Bijoya'r Ghugni
Spicy yellow peas in gravy

Ghugni is another street favourite and this delicious snack is closely linked to Bijoya, the last day of Durga Pujo, when the people of Bengal drown their sorrow by making jars of narkel naru and vats full of ghugni.

My father's family was settled outside Bengal and our Durga Pujo was almost always celebrated with this extended family. My Durga Pujo is therefore reminiscent of the stentorian voice of the priest reciting 'Ya Devi Sarvabhuteshu…' interspersed with an earnest 'Pappu, tum jahan kahi bhi ho…' from a Bihari mother trying to find her son in the pandal crowd. After the goddess had been immersed in the Ganga on Dashami, we celebrated Bijoya for the next few days. To me, Bijoya meant visiting my father's numerous uncles and aunts, touching the elders' feet and then toying around with a plate full of sweets and savouries that did not necessarily make a kid swoon in ecstasy.

There would be plain white china plates with spongy rosogolla, the syrup mixing with the crispy chanachur nestled on the side, homemade nimki, sweet goja and narkel naru. I did not care much for any of this, unless there were samosas or locally made potato chips with their uneven edges, stuff that was taboo at home. Surprisingly, there was no ghugni, or at least none that I remember.

The ghugni I remember was eaten after the Pujo vacation when we had come home after Lokhhi Pujo. School had reopened and there was homework to be done. Amidst this bustle, Ma wanted me to visit the neighbourhood kakus and kakimas to pay my respects. I was not too eager, but I went. The kakimas were always too kind, they wouldn't let me go without plying me with all kinds of food. There were leftover nimkis from Pujo, bereft of any crunch, and narus that had seen better days. Then one of them brought out ghugni, the kind I dreaded, the kind she had probably made in a large quantity and in minimal time. The yellow peas had not been given time to amalgamate with the spices; the gravy was watery, flowing freely on the plate while the stubborn peas sat tight. A spoonful of that and you would hate ghugni for life.

But ghugni is so intertwined with Bong culture that it is not easy to let go of it. And there are better ghugnis in this world, trust me, like the kind Ma makes. So, several years later, I took my first step, steeled my mind and poured pounds of chickpeas into the pressure cooker. Before I could catch my breath and say 'La Bamba', the peas had turned to mush. I promptly chucked them, took out my canned chickpeas and made a ghugni that was quick, easy and super tasty. But connoisseurs turned up their noses and my mother said anything made with canned chickpeas is not a ghugni. Also I had to stick to yellow peas or matar.

I tried it again. This time I soaked the peas and cooked them on the open flame for hours till they reached just the right softness. The ghugni turned out to be delicious, the buttery smoothness of the peas flecked with the right amount of spiciness. It melted in your mouth with every spoon. Everyone was happy and I am now a convert. Over time I have learned to cook the peas correctly in the pressure cooker and that has made life easier.

There are simpler ghugnis than this one, without the onion and with a simple phoron of chilli and whole cumin seeds. There are exotic ones with minced meat and coconut. Some ghugnis have cubed potatoes in them. All of them taste great if you do it right. The traditional ghugni does not have tamarind chutney, or at least, my mother's doesn't. The fennel powder I have used here might raise some Bong eyebrows but it was suggested by a friend's mother and it goes to show how differently the same dish can be made in various Bengali homes.

2 cups dry yellow peas/ matar/white vatana	½ tsp bhaja masala (see page 222)
1 cup finely chopped onion	Salt to taste + ¼ tsp rock salt to finish
1 tbsp ginger paste	
5 green chilli, chopped or slit	¼ tsp sugar
Half a lime	2 tbsp vegetable oil
¼ tsp mouri/fennel powder (optional)	**For garnish**
1 tsp Kashmiri mirch	1–2 tbsp tamarind chutney (see page 217)
½ tsp red chilli powder	Chopped onion, coriander leaves and green chilli for garnish
1 tsp turmeric powder	

♪ Soak the peas overnight. By the next morning they will have swollen in volume. Rinse well, add salt, red chilli powder, turmeric powder and double the water and cook in the pressure cooker for 5 minutes at full pressure. The peas should be soft by now. If you are using canned chickpeas, skip this step.

Note: Chickpeas are not the same as dry yellow peas. Bengali ghugni is made with dry yellow peas but in absence of this you can substitute chickpeas.

♪ Heat oil in a deep pan.

♪ Add finely chopped red onion and sauté till it turns a shade of pinkish brown. This takes 4 minutes. Add ginger paste and green chilli. Add fennel powder and Kashmiri mirch and fry with a sprinkle of water for a couple more minutes till you see the oil separating.

♪ Add the cooked peas along with the water, a little at a time and mix well. Once you have added all the peas, sauté for 2–3 minutes. Add little more water if needed, salt and sugar to taste and cook till peas are soft and the gravy is thick. This will happen quickly since the peas are already cooked. Don't overcook or the skin of the peas will come off. The process will take a little more time for canned chickpeas. I don't like watery ghugni so I dry off most of the water.

♪ Once done squeeze lime juice and add rock salt. Sprinkle bhaja masala. Let it sit to soak in the flavours.

♪ While serving, drizzle tamarind chutney on the ghugni and garnish with finely chopped red onion and coriander leaves.

Note: You can use the tamarind date chutney in this book. If possible, chop the white meaty portions of a coconut into small pieces and add to the ghugni as a garnish.

The Cumin Coriander Tales

Cumin, the brown, dusky seeds used rampantly in Indian cooking, is a staple in the Bengali kitchen too. Along with the whole seeds, cumin powder or jeere guro is much in demand. Instead of buying cumin powder from the grocers, it is best to make your own from the seeds. It takes very little effort and you can make enough to last half a year. I usually lightly roast the cumin seeds and then grind them to make a potent powder.

The straw-yellow round coriander seed is a close friend of the cumin. Where there is one, the other is often to be found as well. I make coriander powder just as I do cumin and I make enough at one go to last me six months.

Ma used dhone-jeere bata in her cooking, a wet paste of cumin and coriander made on the sil-batta. The taste that this paste imparted is distinct from the cumin coriander powder that we use today. But then, we compromise in favour of comfort.

Ten years ago, it was my first Durga Pujo in this country. I was fresh off the boat, did not know any other Bengalis here, and by September I could smell orange-stalked shiuli in the cold air, which only had a hint of maple and roasted hazelnut coffee. I even heard the drumbeats of the dhaak early one morning when there were only cars on the highway. Clearly I was hallucinating.

I did not even know if this goddamn country had a Durga Pujo. Sitting in Kolkata, Ma seemed to know better than I did. She would rattle off names of probash er pujo in the various US cities. She would tell me about Baby mashi's second son, who lived in California and whose wife was chief fundraiser or some such for the Bay Area Pujo. To me it made no sense. I didn't know a soul of whom I could ask these questions.

I was desperate. I had no social life. I wanted to go home.

For the longest time, Durga Pujo to me was about waiting for the holidays, for a train ride to my Baba's home town, for new clothes and sarees for the family, for suitcases musty and mouldy from the attic, about telling the doodhwala that he need not add water to our milk for ten whole days in October; and it was about lots of planning, arguments and packing. On Panchami we would wake up when the skies were still dark, bolt every door with thick padlocks, place our suitcases and hold-alls onto two rickshaws and with the remains of sleep in our eyes, reach the station. Ten days later when we came back from our holiday, everything would be the same except for the anticipation, which was now gone.

So more than the Pujo itself, it was the anticipation and excitement that enamoured me. That part of the equation was missing here.

Finally, in my desperation and aspiration of finding more Bongs in the area who might know about local Pujo, I joined a chat room for Bengalis called 'CalcuttaChat'. This was before the days of Orkut and Facebook. A friend had suggested the site which she had used extensively in her grad school days for Bangali adda. 'It is okay, nothing voyeuristic,' she assured me.

I got sucked in. Click, click, ka-boom.

I became 'BongoMeye' in a virtual place that felt very much like Montu-da's canteen, minus the cha and chop. Lots of people whose social life was in the dumps (like mine) and who probably whiled away lonely evenings drinking cheap wine (not like mine) were out there, shrouded by monikers.

Most of the time that I spent in that chat room, I remained silent, until a recipe of narkel naru was passed around. The frozen grated coconut at the Indian stores made the best narkel naru, the user said. This was news to me. I had always seen Ma grate the tough coconut into a fluffy, sweet cloud and then cook it with brown jaggery to make her naru.

The fact that I could use frozen grated coconut to make the same delicious sweet perked me up. And that is how I became friendly with Sudha, her name on screen. The name, unlike most others on the forum, was plain, simple and unadorned. She was like the mashima waiting for an audience, any audience, to talk to about her arthritic right knee. Only, she did not talk about her own knee, she asked after mine. Considerate, always helpful, suggesting I put a little javitri in my garam masala and buy Golden temple atta for my chakki-fresh roti, she was always just a ping away. It turned out she lived in the same area as we did and hence knew everything possible about the neighbourhood Durga Pujo, Lokkhi Pujo, Kali Pujo, Amabashya, Purnima, the works. Armed with all the information I had obtained from her, the H-man and I were ready to go to the three-day weekend Durga Pujo that very week.

She had also expressed a desire to meet me. 'I will be dressed in white and standing by the stall that sells sarees,' she had said. I agreed, eager to meet my lifeline.

Freshly bathed and wrapped in a five-metre silk wonder, I was all excited to be at the Durga Pujo in the school auditorium that weekend. The H-man did not share my enthusiasm, but trudged along.

At the mandap we were bedazzled. Blinded would be more appropriate, actually. We failed to see the goddess. Our eyes were plastered to heavy gold jewellery, intricate gold necklaces, beautiful women and expensive bomkais. I didn't know a single soul and felt out of place. No longer did I want a happening social life. I wanted to get back to my one-bedroom apartment and watch *F.R.I.E.N.D.S.*

After the anjali, I chickened out. I did not want to meet Sudha, who probably had a 2-foot-long gold chain and coiffed hair. But just before we left, I couldn't resist a peek at the saree stall where we were supposed to meet. Instead of a genteel lady in her fifties, I saw a middle-aged man dressed in a white chikan kurta-pajama, clearly waiting for someone.

I never logged onto CalcuttaChat again. Since then I have made many friends where I live and made many desserts, but 'Sudha's' tip for narkel naru has stood by me all these years.

Love in the Time of Dessert

'Forget love... I would rather fall in a rosogulla syrup,' said the Bong girl to her fiancé.

It was a Tuesday in December, a week before Christmas, and everyone's wish for a white Christmas had been granted, only a bit early. The snow that had inched up over the weekend was no longer white; murky brown would describe it better. That did not lower anyone's spirits, at least not the 'spirit of buying'. Stores were milling with people scrambling to get the last pair of juicy couture wedges in neon pink (on sale). Hot chocolate, tired Santas in the mall and a continuous onslaught of 'Have a holly jolly Christmas' on my car radio constantly reminded me of the Christmas frenzy. There was no way one could escape.

It is not that I wanted to escape. I love Christmas. Years of Catholic school has pumped nativity scenes into my blood. All my childhood, my very Hindu grandparents along with the rest of the family celebrated Christmas in our special way. I gave everyone – everyone – a handmade card with a picture of a waxing candle and red poinsettias. My grandma mistook those red flowers for hibiscus and thought Jesus loved 'joba phul'. On 25 December every year, she picked two extra hibiscuses from her tree and put them in her pujo room for Christ. My grandfather got fruit cakes wrapped in yellow cellophane and dotted with red-green tutti fruties to celebrate the birth of the son of God. They did not think he was the son of God. But that did not matter. Christmas was a good day, one that you celebrated with desserts. The same logic applied to Eid, Shitola Shoshthi, Holi, Ramadan and anything in between.

Now, however, I had more important things to plan for. It was my eldest's birthday the next day. Birthdays are important around here; parties, goodie bags, frosted cakes, the whole zing-bang. 'When I am four, I will be new. Now I am old,' says my three year old, wistfully eyeing her sister's birthday preparations. But before any of that, I had to make paayesh.

In a repeat performance of my traditional 'let's-buy-the-most-important-stuff-at-the-last-minute', I had to ditch my Zumba class for a trip to the grocery store. A litre of milk, a quart of Half-n-Half and golden California raisins – I checked them off the list in my head. For the small grained rice I would have to go all the way to the Indian grocery on the other side of town. Plodding around in the snow in high boots was really not my fantasy and I hoped to find the last packet of Gobindobhog rice in my pantry. At least I had the patali, the deep brown, sweet smelling khejur gur saved from my last Kolkata trip.

I was confident. The paayesh would be done in an hour tonight. I would still have time to bake a cake. My older daughter doesn't care for paayesh and probably wouldn't go beyond the single mandatory spoonful. I still make it year after year, just like my mother did. Paayesh on birthdays is a tradition I like to follow. I had slowly gotten better at it and could probably do it blindfolded, going by the fragrance at various stages. I knew my paayesh would turn out just right, creamy and sweet, the rice just enough to give the milk company but never to overpower it.

A few years ago I was dead scared of making paayesh. In my grandparents' home, making paayesh was a sacred affair. It was made only on rare occasions that needed some celebration. And that meant only birthdays and Lokkhi Pujo. It wasn't looked upon as a dessert to be served to guests after a lavish meal. Instead it was treated in accordance with its name – 'Paramanna', the food for gods. Cooked only for the family with as much piousness as is usually reserved for chanting the Gayatri mantra, it was a solemn dish.

My ma, the accomplished cook, would actually be quite jittery on the days she cooked paayesh. The standards to which her paayesh would be held were enormous. Baba strongly believed (and still does, even now at 70) that his grandmother, Boro ma, made the best paayesh. 'Thakuma'r moton paayesh keu banate pare na,' he thinks that no one can make a paayesh sweetened with kheju gur like Boro ma.

During winter, especially January, in the villages of Bengal, the sweet smelling sap from the date palm trees is harvested fresh and that juice is made into a jaggery called khejur gur, also known as nolen gur or patali gur. Its colour is a deep rich brown like freshly hoed earth after the rains. My father's grandmother sourced her jaggery from the farmers. Sometimes she would buy it from a villager who would come all the way in to town, selling the gur loaded on his bicycle. There would be liquid khejur gur, in earthen pots, as well as solid rounds of patali. Each rounded block would be scrutinized, smelled and then selected by Boro ma with as much care as was lavished on a fine zardosi from the saree shop.

Once the jaggery had been obtained, the first chaaler paayesh, rice kheer, of the season would be cooked with a few grains of the new rice and the fragrant patali. The more liquid version of jaggery would be served with roti or paratha or soft white dosa-like soru chakli. Boro ma would sit in the kitchen, at the far end of the house, hovering over a large brass pot of milk on the clay stove. I guess the flickering embers in the stove kept her warm on those cold winter afternoons. There was a lot of milk, a lot of family. Every now and then, Baba, or one of his cousins, would be entrusted with the work of stirring the milk with a long brass ladle. The milk needed to be babysat, to be stoked, cajoled, and stirred. This could go on for much longer than an hour and the more eager hands volunteered, the better. Only once the milk had turned a thick creamy white with touches of faint pink and the rice in the milk had been cooked, the paayesh was taken off the heat. Crumbled pieces of brown palm jaggery, enchantingly aromatic, were now added to it. The fragrance of that paayesh was so enticing that the surroundings reverberated in its aroma.

'The milk has to be thick to be just right, it shouldn't flow freely when its little droplets hit a flat surface, but neither can it be thick and starchy like a pudding,' says Ma.

I have never had the good fortune to taste my Boro ma's paayesh. Over the years, my baba has agreed that my mother's paayesh is very much like his grandmother's. Tastes ebb and flow and then one day you are not sure whether the taste you are talking of rests on your tongue or in your memory. The day he said my paayesh tasted just like Ma's I knew I had nailed it.

I don't own a pair of Manolo Blahnik's, but I knew I had arrived.

Khejur Gurer Paayesh
Paayesh with palm jaggery

1½ litre whole milk
½ litre Half & Half milk
  Note: Ma uses 2 litres of
  whole milk only. I use the Half
  & Half as it reduces my effort
  to thicken the milk.
2/3 cup Gobindobhog rice or
  basmati rice
½ tsp ghee, enough to smear
  the rice with
  A fistful of raisins soaked in
  water

3 bay leaves
1 cup sugar
1 cup khejur gur/date palm
  jaggery
Note: the sugar and khejur gur
  amounts to almost 2 cups.
  This is sweet enough for me.
  Between the sugar and gur
  you can increase one and
  decrease the other.

ɔ̀ Wash the rice, drain the water and then smear the rice grains with
  a little ghee.

ɔ̀ Pour both kinds of milk in a boiling pan, usually a deep, heavy-
  bottomed pan. I use a deep non-stick one. Add 3 or 4 bay leaves.
  Let the milk come to a boil. Be careful so that the milk does not
  boil over.

ɔ̀ When the milk comes to a boil, add the rice. Stir intermittently
  and check if the rice is done. You have to keep stirring frequently,
  else the milk might scald the bottom of the pan as it thickens.

ɔ̀ When the rice is cooked, add the sugar.

Note: Adding sugar before the rice has boiled hinders its getting cooked
properly. Now stir the milk continuously so that the milk does not burn
or scald the bottom of the container and the rice does not stick. You also
need to be careful that it does not boil over. So keep a watch.

♪ When the milk has thickened to the right consistency (to check
   this, take a spoonful of liquid and pour it on a flat plate; the
   viscosity of the milk should be such that it does not flow freely),
   switch off the heat. By this time the milk would have also reduced
   from its original volume. The time taken to reach this stage is
   around an hour or so.

♪ Take the paayesh off the heat and add the khejur gur after 5
   minutes. Stir well. Add gur, depending on your desired sweetness
   level.

   *Note: If your gur or jaggery has been refrigerated, put it in the microwave
   to soften. Savour the sweet smell of khejur gur. It is pure bliss. The gur
   has to be added only after the paayesh is taken off the heat. Adding gur
   to hot milk may curdle it.*

♪ Add the plumped up raisins. Serve hot or cold. The paayesh
   thickens a little more on cooling. I like it better cold.

Reviving Those Darn Traditions

I am not a winter person. I don't like bitter cold, cockroaches
and broccoli cheddar soup in that order. Skiing, snow-
tubing or even building a snowman does not ignite fire in
my belly. Nah, I am a brown, warm person from the tropics
and I would like to remain that way.

In January, when the wine from the New Year's party has
worn off and resolutions have been overlooked, I raise the
thermostat to 70 degrees Fahrenheit, crank up the fireplace,
dress myself in crumpled yoga pants and huddle on my
corner of the couch. I have no wish to lift my derriere from
the spot and let it go cold.

'Cook your egg curry.'

'Warm up the pasta.'

'Let's just have Cheerios for dinner.'

These are the words I spout at the H-man. After the third sentence, he invariably walks to the kitchen and starts chopping onions for a dim kosha.

Last January was no different. Even 14 January was exactly the same as 13 January. And I was sitting in my favourite spot, trying to think up sensual lines that would send the H-man to the kitchen.

Until, that is, my seven-year-old's Tam-Bram friend dropped in for a playdate. It was bitter cold outside and my daughter was clearly elated by the arrangement.

'Happy Sankranti, Aunty!' the little mite said, pulling off her faux Ugg boots and triple layered jacket.

Poush Sankranti? Today? So that must be why Ma-in-law called in the morning. Good that I didn't pick up the phone.

'What did you make, Aunty? My mother made chakkarai pongal, ven pongal and vadais,' she continued.

'Huh, when did your analyst mom morph into an Iyengar maami in her nine yard silks?' I grumbled to myself.

To the kids I announced, 'Well, we are going to make pithey now. And also patishapta,' and pulled my fat derriere away from the snug, comfortable couch. Anything to uphold the Bong pride on Sankranti.

'Pithey, really? How can you make pithey, Mommy? Pithey means back, right?' My daughter was bewildered.

The kid was familiar with only one meaning of pithey in the Bengali language, which meant the back of the human body. She had no clue about the sweeter meaning of the word, a dessert that is strongly associated with the harvest festival and made on Sankranti or Poush Parbon.

Her ignorance was totally my fault. I rarely ever made pithey. And then again, you did not make a pithey at any random time of the year. It had to be in mid-January on and around the day of Sankranti, when rural Bengal celebrates Poush Parbon or Poush Sankranti, a harvest festival. The freshly harvested paddy and the khejur gur is used to make many sweets like the different varieties of pithey on this day.

My thamma, my dad's mother, was not very enthusiastic about Sankranti and did not encourage devoting time to making or eating pithey on Poush Parbon. She made a great paayesh and notun gur er paayesh was the only sweet that got cooked on Sankranti in my paternal grandparents' home in Bihar.

I was never too fond of pithey either, and remember Sankranti as days of excruciating cold in the plains where winter was usually mild. The cold winds from the north would rustle through the green leaves of the guava tree in the garden, making the cotton quilts inadequate. In the absence of central heating, the only warmth would come from the mid-day sun. Bath water would be heated in big colanders and a kettle always hissed on the dying embers of the clay stove. To soak up the sun, we would sit on the terrace, huddled in hand-knit sweaters, our freshly washed hair strewn across our backs, the golden sun streaming down on us.

The few winters that we spent at my Dida's home in Kolkata, Poush Sankranti shone with its fervor. Dida celebrated every small and big festival listed in the Bengali almanac in the manner she knew best – through food. Poush Sankranti in her home was a three-day affair with sweet and savoury pitheys of all kinds imaginable. She would store the first batch of ashkey pithey in an earthenware container as a symbolic offering to the gods and later immerse it in the river. Then there would be half-moon shaped puli pithey soaking in sweetened thick milk, gokul pithey stuffed with kheer and dunked in syrup, ranga alu'r pithey made of the fresh harvest of sweet potatoes, nonta pithey which would be stuffed with green peas and coconut and thin lacy crepes called patishapta. My grandfather would beckon to all and sundry to come and have a taste of the wonderful sweets and my poor, harried Dida would rush about grating, grinding, stuffing and frying. Ma and my aunts revived that tradition later, making sure that at least three different kinds of pithey were made at Sankranti. I was lax until I realized how a piece of fried sweetened dough on Sankranti could link my daughter to her roots.

The girls were hyper at the prospect of helping me make pithey. I decided on patishapta instead. It was easier for their made-in-the-USA palate. And honestly, it was easier for me too. Why I cannot serve it at any other time of the year I don't know. Remind me, I should ask the Ma-in-law.

Patishapta
Crepes with a coconut-kheer stuffing

For the pur or stuffing:

3   cups grated coconut

12   oz khoa

1   cup sugar. Using date palm
jaggery would be the best.

For the batter:

1   cup maida/all purpose flour

1/6   cup sooji/semolina

2   tsp sugar

2   cups milk. Start with
1½ cups and then reserve
½ cup to be added gradually
if needed.

Note: The batter needs to be really thin and you may need more milk for this. Ideally, the batter should spread easily on the griddle when poured.

To make the coconut-kheer stuffing:

♪ Take the grated coconut. Fresh is better, but I also use frozen. Microwave the frozen one to make it soft and fluffy. In the kadhai or frying pan, mix the grated coconut with sugar and mix by hand, pressing a little, so that the coconut becomes slightly moist because of the sugar. This step is taken before the pan is put on the stove.

♪ Next, microwave the khoa to soften it.

♪ Put the kadhai/frying pan with coconut mix in it on the stove and stir. Add the khoa and keep on stirring till the mixture turns a light brown and is sticky. At this point, the mix should not disintegrate but should look like a light brown slightly sticky granular substance. It takes almost 30 minutes to achieve this result.

To make the crepes:

♪ Put the maida, sooji and sugar in a wide-mouthed bowl. Mix lightly with a fork.

♪ Add about 1½ cups milk and mix well to get a smooth batter. If the batter is thick and not of a pourable consistency, you need to thin it down. Now slowly add the remaining ½ cup milk or water, mixing it till you get the right consistency of batter. The batter should be a little more liquid than pancake batter.

♪ Heat a frying pan and smear a little oil/ghee on it, about ½ tsp should be fine. I prefer to use a non-stick frying pan for this as that makes cleaning up easier.

♪ Take a ladle (about ¼ cup) full of batter and pour it on the frying pan. Tilting the pan and spreading the mixture with back of the ladle, evenly distribute the batter in a circle. You have to do this quickly before the mix sets. This step will be a breeze if you have made dosas. You might need to add a few drops of oil around the edges for easy removal of the crepes.

♪ In about 3 minutes at medium heat you will see the edges turning crisp and the centre will look cooked. Put the stuffing lengthwise at the centre of the crepe. Fold the crepe and when it browns a little, take it out. The measure given here will make about 10–12 crepes.

For serving:
♪ Drizzle the crepes with condensed milk and serve hot. Ideally, Ma would thicken the milk, sweeten it and pour it over the crepes. I cut the method short with condensed milk. You can also drizzle the liquid patali gur which is in season during Sankranti. I make do with maple syrup.

NARKEL NARU
Coconut laddoos

My policy regarding desserts is to desert them if they take longer than thirty minutes to prepare. So I am always on the lookout for simple desserts that can be further simplified. The narkel naru is the perfect example. It is made very often at home for the various pujos that dot the calendar and is a must during Kojagari Lokkhi Pujo on the day of the full moon that follows Durga Pujo. The evening before, my mother, her help and an aunt would sit down to grate the coconut on a curved iron boti with a special blade for grating. I watched, awed as with the rhythmic movement of their hands, mounds of soft, sweet, cloudy coconut meat gathered on the newspaper. Later, when the Anjali brand of kitchenware was introduced, they had a table-top coconut grater where you turned a handle which in turn rotated a blade that grated the coconut. That instrument was deemed fit for me and I was entrusted with the task of using it while the elders used the boti.

However, grating the coconut takes away a whole lot of time and joy from making the naru. The frozen grated coconut that I get here in the US brought me back that joy. With a pack of that, the naru gets done very, very quickly. If you are in no-freeze land, and do not get frozen grated coconut, I am sure you can get hold of some human who will help you with the grating. From there, life and narkel naru becomes an easy journey.

Makes about 20 narus/laddoos

3 cups grated coconut. I have used the frozen MTR brand, you can grate and use fresh coconut. When using the frozen product, thaw before use.

1 cup sugar

½ tsp ground cardamom seeds

2 cups evaporated milk. If using whole milk, you need to reduce 3 cups of milk to 2 cups.

¼ cup condensed milk. You can skip this and increase the sugar, but I prefer this.

꒷ In a deep, heavy-bottomed pan mix the coconut and sugar by hand thoroughly.

꒷ Put the pan on low heat and then stir for 4 to 5 minutes. The sugar will melt and mix with the coconut and the coconut will be lightly roasted. Add milk and condensed milk to the above. Add some ground cardamom.

꒷ Mix it all together and cook at low to medium heat with frequent stirring till the coconut is cooked. This will take some time so don't panic. Keep stirring till the milk is almost dried up and the coconut mix comes out clean from the sides. You will know by the slight change in colour and the fact that the mix will no longer stick to the pan. Don't dry it too much, else you cannot make the balls.

Note: When you think it is almost done, test it out by trying to make a ball that stays in shape. The approximate time to reach this stage is 30–40 minutes at medium heat.

꒷ Take the pan off the heat and cool it slightly. When the mix is still warm to touch, make balls by rolling it between your palms. Store in an air-tight container. I usually refrigerate my narus, but Ma used to keep them out.

MALPUA

Malpua is another sweet that Ma would make for Bijoya after Durga Pujo. She would also make it on occasions like Holi and sometimes with sweet potatoes at Sankranti. I loved these soft, sugar-soaked delicacies. However, I liked them crisp and just a tad soaked in the syrup. Baba, on the other hand, liked them soaked and almost breaking apart in the syrup. So I would eat them fast within the first few minutes while they were still hot and crisp. For Baba, the malpuas would be left in their soaking sugar bath to be had later. So you can take your pick on how and when to eat them. It is delicious, any which way.

For the malpua batter:	To make sugar syrup:
½ cup maida/all purpose flour	1 cup water
¼ cup sooji/semolina/rawa	1 cup sugar
1 cup evaporated milk	A few strands of saffron
5 tbsp condensed milk	½ cup white oil for frying
2 tbsp sugar	**To garnish:**
1 tsp saunf/fennel seeds	Slivers of almond
¼ cup golden raisins	

♪ First make the sugar syrup. Boil 1 cup sugar and 1 cup water till you get syrup of one single thread consistency. You can flavour the syrup with strands of saffron or with drops of rose water. A single thread syrup is not very thick and the consistency is right for absorbing. To check, dip a spatula in the syrup and remove. Now, with the tip of your forefinger, carefully touch a drop on the spatula and pull apart slowly with your thumb. It can be hot so be careful. A single thread should stretch between your fingers for a syrup of single thread consistency.

♪ Next make a batter with ingredients listed under 'batter'.

Note: Instead of evaporated milk you can use 1½ cups whole milk that has been reduced to 1 cup.

♪ Throw some golden raisins in the batter and mix. Let the batter sit for 2–3 hours for the best results. Leave it for at least 20 minutes, even if you are in a rush.

♪ Heat oil for deep frying in a kadhai.

♪ Give the batter a good mix and pour a little less than ¼ cup batter in the hot oil to form a circular disc. When the edges turn golden brown, flip and fry till both sides are golden.

♪ Remove with a slotted spoon. Either dunk in sugar syrup or brush both sides generously with the syrup.

Note: If you intend to dunk in sugar syrup till the malpuas are soaked, lessen the sweetness in the batter. I prefer a quick brush with sugar syrup or a quick dunk in the syrup (this is easier). That makes it not very soft, but sweet and slightly crisp.

♪ Garnish with slivers of almond and serve hot. They stay okay for a couple of days when refrigerated, but remember to warm them before serving .These proportions make about 10–12 malpuas.

The Beginning of a Sweet End

It was a November evening, five years ago. The woods were a flaming magenta beyond my kitchen window. The golden orb of light had just plunged into that mass of colour. The days had grown shorter and darkness fell slowly in patches like bountiful fluffs of blackberry cotton candy. The fairy lights put up for the holidays were twinkling on the front porch. I was a mom at the crossroads. I had travelled a long way to reach here and now I had no clue about my directions. My child was two and a half; my career was in a lull; I had found new joy in turning up the stove and chucking paanch-phoron into the hissing oil; I was lost in indecision. Work outside home or stay at home? Part-time or full? In this moment of statelessness, I happened upon a food blog and then two and then many, many more.

I was mesmerized. Amazing things like rhubarb clafoutis, perfect maroon macaroons and buttery quinces stared at

me through the panes of Internet Explorer. Beautiful plates,
pretty countrysides, food set out in a way I might have only
dared to imagine. A sprig of thyme daintily tucked in, a swirl
of cream, a sprinkle of coarse pink salt all done painstakingly
to perfection. People eat like that, even with toddlers tugging
at their aprons? They have rolled up napkins and beautiful
crockery set out on distressed wood tables for a quiet lunch
at home? No one actually gulps down dal and rice, licking
their fingers and standing by the counter, like me? And
everyone has matching sets of spoons to eat with?

My frustrations grew worse. Here I was, trying to get
a toehold in the realm of my very own Bengali cooking
when the world had already passed me by and was serving
lemon curd in exact pairs of matching cups.

Yes, there were umpteen things I could have done to
forget the helplessness, the indecision that comes with
being at the crossroads and checking blogs. I could have
folded clothes, for one. There was a whole load that I hadn't
even taken out of the dryer.

Instead I created an account for myself on Blogger and
started a blog. If I was having fun making aloo posto at
home, I wanted it to be out there on the internet, jostling
with a gorgeous chocolate pavlova. I think these kinds of
destructive thoughts were a side effect of singing 'Mary had
a little lamb' the whole day, but I can't say for sure.

'I want to chronicle the food I cook and eat to pass on
my traditions,' I said. 'This is one more of your pastimes that
you will give up in a week,' the H-man said.

Soon things got out of hand. Someone left a comment
on my post. I went totally crazy. There were actually
people there who wanted to try my aloo posto? While

my cooking was okay and elicited mild enthusiasm from people who ate it, the few people who read my blog went overboard with praise. I mean, here was someone who had not even tasted my kalakand and he/she was going 'Wow', 'gorgeous', 'Awesome'.

Even commenters with suspicious names like 'Buy Viagra' said things like 'Buy Viagra...Very interesting post... something really informative... I wish to read something like this again... we keep coming back to your blog.' In this day and age, who does that?

My faith in humanity was reinstated.

My life took a new turn. Everything I ate, I wanted to post on my blog. I couldn't even eat a single morsel of aloo-seddho bhaat without itching to write about it. What if someone dies of hunger just because they did not know how to make aloo-seddho? What if someone thinks aloo-seddho is the same as mashed potatoes? What if someone forgets all about the mustard oil and green chilli? All I waited for actually was for at least ten people to pop up and say that my aloo-seddho was the best in the world.

My life was guided by my blog. It had found a new meaning, albeit a virtual one.

If the H-man so much as ever suggested that my egg curry could do with more salt, I would go ballistic. 'Salt your own curry,' I would say, not even bothering to pass the salt shaker. But when an anonymous person left a comment asking for how much salt and how much water I put in my gravy, I went to IKEA and bought a set of measuring cups and spoons. I took measurements! A dal that I would have actually cooked in fifteen minutes now took all of forty five. I measured out the oil, vacillated between ¼ tsp and

1/6 tsp kalonji and timed how long it took for the onion to
fry. Instead of a stainless steel kadhai, I asked Ma to get me
a brand new Camel Geometry box on her next trip. She
scorned my request. And then when I gave her a ruler and
asked her to measure the length of ginger for mutton kosha
she switched off the gas and never wanted to hear of my
blog again. Much later she came around, sending me recipes
via e-mail, all perfectly measured and timed.

Barring such adverse side effects, the scenario had its
positive side. I cooked a lot, paid more attention to the finer
points and because of all that effort, I was getting better at
the cooking part.

I also took pictures of the food I cooked. In unnatural
surroundings. Amidst candelabras and forks I never use. I
bought single pieces of battered cutlery at exorbitant prices
online as props for blog photos.

'Nooooo, don't touch that. That white plate with the
etching is only for my blog!' You could hear me scream as
I struggled to take shots of a bubbling maachher jhol. The
family waited patiently while I took shots of the fish from
all possible precarious angles as if it was Malaika Arora and
not maachher jhol.

The worst thing that happened however was my
unforeseen inclination to bake. It drove the household
crazy and upset regular programming. Before I started a
blog, I rarely baked. If I did, it was from a box. A Betty
Crocker tried and tested yellow cake mix was my saviour
on birthdays, anniversaries and Christmas. The cake would
turn out moist, fluffy and perfectly sweet. For the kids, I
would slather on some frosting and dole out a generous
helping of sprinkles.

'You make the best cake ever,' my then three-year-old would say. I had no such fantasies. No one in my family baked fancy cakes. Ma had one of those round aluminum electric ovens that looked like a UFO and she made cake in it twice a year. It was always the same recipe, flour, baking powder, eggs, oil, sugar. And yet there was no knowing how the cake would turn out. On good days, it would rise and live up to the soft fluffiness that a cake demands. On others, the batter would stiffen and be uptight, the cake hard to cut through even with the best intentions. The uncertainty of the whole thing kept me away from baking for a good part of my life.

I decided to change this when I first started blogging. A few months into my blog I settled on an orange muffin as my first baking trial.

I had butter, eggs, flour, oranges and everything else the recipe needed, except for patience. In a hurry, I tried to beat the butter before it had even come to room temperature. So that was a disaster at the start. I had to scrape it from the blades and soften it in the microwave and then beat it.

Then all seemed to go well, and I left the muffins in the oven to bake. They browned and the aroma was splendid. I felt all smug and Paula Deen-ish. But there was a glitch.

The muffins did not rise as they should have. They were very stiff, or stubborn I should say, and did not want to 'rise to the occasion'. They did not realize that hazaar people across the blog world would see them, eye them, make them 'eye candy' if they were worth it, heap praises on them. No, those muffins refused to understand the gravity of the situation and stood stiff like my three year old does sometimes. I can manage her, but the muffins – nope. My coaxing, cajoling, my promise to give them other muffins if they were good, all of it fell flat.

So like worried parents we (yes, both me and the H-man) sat down to dissect their behavior. What made them do this – was it us, the environment, the society, their upbringing, what? We went through the recipe again and it seemed like we had done all that was asked for. Yes, I was a bit tense, and did mutter a curse or two but I swear that was in hushed undertones. I did beat the butter and the eggs and the flour but that's what was asked for, no one said anything about 'not beating'. These were muffins, not my child.

Finally it dawned on us. Instead of the baking soda, I had used baking powder in the recipe. Who cares? Apparently muffins do.

It has been almost four years since that first failed trial. I have had a number of such attempts where the cake did not rise or the batter stuck to the sheet or it tasted so crummy that we had to throw the whole thing out. Instead of baking a perfect cake on those occasions, I have excelled at a bhapa ilish or a sugary malpua instead.

As I have improved my baking, I have also learned to let go. There is no point in doing everything and expecting to come out the best. One has to choose the path they want to take. Years ago, I had involuntarily taken a decision to be there for my daughters, to give them a warm, homecooked meal, to feed them and raise them well.

Today I am still working on my promise. Tomorrow, as they grow older, that promise might also include perfectly baked cakes. We will see.

For now, 'Be End' – as my youngest would say, and happy cooking to you all!

Spices Translated

Asafoetida	*Hing*	Helps in digestion, just what you need
Bay leaf or Indian bay leaf	*Tej pata*	Aromatic, anti-inflammatory and treats sore throat
Black cardamom	*Boro elaichi*	Has smoky flavor and might treat stomach disorders
Caraway seeds	*Shah zeera*	Pungent, anise-like flavor and used for stomach complaints
Cinnamon	*Dalchini or Daruchini*	Widely used in home remedies for cold and flu
Clove	*Lobongo or Laung*	Along with cinnamon, clove is also used to treat throat troubles
Coriander	*Dhone*	Works on your digestive and respiratory system
Cumin	*Jeere*	Kindles appetite and helps in digestion
Fennel	*Mouri or Saunf*	Cooling spice that helps in digestion

Fenugreek seeds	*Methi seeds*	These seeds have loads of benefits and digestion is one amongst many
Green cardamom	*Chhoto elaichi*	Prevents throat troubles. And that is why you want it in your tea
Mace	*Joitri or Javetri*	Known for its anti-oxidant, anti-depressant and digestive properties
Mustard oil	*Shorshe dana or Rai*	Anti-bacterial, anti-fungal, digestive aid
Nigella seeds	*Kalo jeere or Kalonji*	Has many medicinal qualities
Nutmeg	*Jaiphal*	Known for its stimulant, carminative and astringent properties
Poppy seeds	*Posto*	Is highly nutritious and has anti-oxidant properties
Saffron	*Zafran*	This beautiful spice is a good remedy for liver enlargement and kidney infection
Turmeric	*Holud*	This everyday spice strengthens your immune system and is a powerful anti-oxidant

Acknowledgements

In no particular order, this book happened because of:

Ma, who fed me well, still does, and believes 'a girl does not need to learn to cook'. All because of you.

Baba, who reads my food blog diligently even though he couldn't give a hoot about cooking.

My husband, who chops vegetables, does the dishes, criticizes my food, eats it and taught me all about 'oil separating from masala'. He also read every single draft of this book until he was tired of it. You are the best.

My two daughters Sharanya and Ananya, who know their cumin from their coriander, love jhol as much as pasta and have no clue why I am writing this book. Hopefully one day they will.

My Dida, who instilled in me a love for traditional Bengali cooking. Only, I found it rather late. My Boromama, who always believed in my omelette.

My in-laws, who make legendary dim kosha and more. My sis-in-law Paroma, who shares her excellent recipes when I need them most.

Thamma, Kaku-Kakima, mashis, cousins and everyone in my extended family who never thought I would cook. Eat? Yes. Cook? No.

BFF's Nandini and Rumi, thanks for being there. And for everything else.

Mumu–Kaushik, Tapasi–Ranada, who eat and praise anything I attempt to cook. And feed me when I don't.

My lovely erudite editor Neelini Sarkar, who believed there was a book in my blog, helped shape it and guided me through the maze of the publishing world. Achala, Shuka, Nitesh, Jojy and the team at HarperCollins who worked as hard as me on this book. It is as much their baby as mine. Okay, mine a little more.

My blogosphere pals, Miri, Mandira, Manisha, Indosungod, Sravanthi, Vani, Nupur, Miss Masala Mallika, Finla, Cham, Cynthia, Sigma, Sailu, Anita, Linda, Jaya W, Jaya M, Soma, Pree, Sharmila, Mallika di, Ushnish da and Kalyan, to name a few who inspire.

My friends here in the US, Anamitra, Jayeeta, Jaya, Moumita, Room, Tina, Moushumi, Nabanita, Sharmishtha and Baishali, who conjure elaborate feasts.

And most importantly, the readers who visit my blog, try out my recipes and thus gave me the courage to write this book.

Download the QR code reader and scan this code with your smartphone to discover more delicious recipes on the Bong Mom's blog.